CHRISTMAS GIFTS OF GOOD TASTE

*C*hristmas comes but once a year, and with it comes the time-honored tradition of gift-giving. What better way to show you care than to offer delicious homemade goodies in merry packages that you make yourself! In this edition of Christmas Gifts of Good Taste *we present a new and exciting collection of inventive ideas for all your friends and family. Using just a little of your time and creativity, you can delight everyone on your list with eye-catching offerings, including a kids' snack mix delivered in a toy truck or purse and a cheery popcorn snowman dressed in a top hat and a licorice scarf! Show loved ones how much they mean to you by sharing tokens of kindness made especially for them — uniquely by you.*

Anne Childs

LEISURE ARTS, INC.
Little Rock, Arkansas

CHRISTMAS GIFTS of GOOD TASTE

EDITORIAL STAFF

Vice President and Editor-in-Chief: Anne Van Wagner Childs
Executive Director: Sandra Graham Case
Design Director: Patricia Wallenfang Sowers
Test Kitchen Director/Foods Editor: Celia Fahr Harkey, R.D.
Editorial Director: Susan Frantz Wiles
Publications Director: Kristine Mertes
Creative Art Director: Gloria Bearden
Senior Graphics Art Director: Melinda Stout

DESIGN
Designers: Katherine Prince Horton, Sandra Spotts Ritchie, Linda Diehl Tiano, Rebecca Sunwall Werle, and Anne Pulliam Stocks
Executive Assistant: Billie Steward

FOODS
Assistant Foods Editor: Jane Kenner Prather
Test Kitchen Home Economist: Rose Glass Klein
Test Kitchen Coordinator: Nora Faye Taylor
Test Kitchen Assistants: Camille T. Alstadt and Tanya Harris Yates

TECHNICAL
Managing Editor: Barbara McClintock Vechik
Technical Writers: Jennifer L. Hobbs and Susan McManus Johnson

EDITORIAL
Managing Editor: Linda L. Trimble
Associate Editor: Stacey Robertson Marshall
Assistant Editors: Terri Leming Davidson and Janice Teipen Wojcik

ART
Book/Magazine Graphics Art Director: Diane M. Hugo
Senior Production Graphics Artist: Michael A. Spigner
Photography Stylist: Karen Smart Hall

PROMOTIONS
Managing Editors: Alan Caudle and Marjorie Ann Lacy
Associate Editors: Debby Carr, Ellen J. Clifton, Steven M. Cooper, and Dixie L. Morris
Designer: Dale Rowett
Art Director: Linda Lovette Smart
Production Artist: Leslie Loring Krebs
Publishing Systems Administrator: Cynthia M. Lumpkin
Publishing Systems Assistants: Susan Mary Gray and Robert Walker

BUSINESS STAFF

Publisher: Rick Barton
Vice President and General Manager: Thomas L. Carlisle
Vice President, Finance: Tom Siebenmorgen
Vice President, Retail Marketing: Bob Humphrey
Vice President, National Accounts: Pam Stebbins
Retail Marketing Director: Margaret Sweetin
General Merchandise Manager: Cathy Laird

Vice President, Operations: Brian U. Davis
Distribution Director: Rob Thieme
Retail Customer Service Director: Tonie B. Maulding
Retail Customer Service Managers: Carolyn Pruss and Wanda Price
Print Production Manager: Fred F. Pruss

Library of Congress Catalog Number 98-65190
International Standard Book Number 1-57486-120-4

Table of Contents

*T*o share favorite recipes with relatives or wonderful friends, present them with our handy recipe kit displayed in a charming basket. Snuggle in a jar of our Honey-Raspberry Glaze to use as a basting sauce or as a complement for meats. Be sure to include the recipe — they'll want to pass the delicacy on to other special pals!

HONEY-RASPBERRY GLAZE

- $1/2$ cup minced onion
- 1 clove garlic, minced
- 1 jalapeño pepper, seeded and finely chopped
- 2 tablespoons olive oil
- 2 cans (8 ounces each) tomato sauce
- 1 jar (12 ounces) seedless raspberry jam
- $1/4$ cup Worcestershire sauce
- $1/4$ cup honey
- $1/2$ teaspoon salt
- $1/2$ teaspoon ground black pepper

In a large saucepan, sauté onion, garlic, and jalapeño pepper in oil over medium heat until vegetables are tender. Stir in tomato sauce, jam, Worcestershire sauce, honey, salt, and black pepper. Reduce heat to medium-low and simmer uncovered 30 minutes. Spoon glaze into heat-resistant jars; cover and cool to room temperature. Store in refrigerator. Use as a basting sauce for poultry or meat.

Yield: about 3 cups glaze

"FAMILY RECIPES" GIFT SET

BASKET
You will need a basket (we used an 11" dia. basket), 1"w satin ribbon, glue, 1" dia. button, and fabric for liner.

1. Measure around basket; add 8". Cut a length of ribbon the determined measurement. Knot ribbon around basket; glue button to knot.
2. Follow *Making a Basket Liner*, page 123, to make liner with an unfinished edge.

RECIPE BOOK
You will need an 8"w x $9^1/4$"h x 2"d photo album with center rings and 4" x 6" photo sleeves, kitchen-motif fabric to cover album, batting, poster board, light-colored fabric for album label, paper-backed fusible web, tracing paper, transfer paper, black permanent medium-point marker, 1"w satin ribbon, and three 1" dia. buttons.

1. Cut one $11^1/4$" x 20" piece of fabric and one $9^1/4$" x 18" piece of batting. With album closed, glue batting to outside of album.
2. Center open album on wrong side of fabric piece. Fold corners of fabric diagonally over corners of album; glue in place. Fold short edges of fabric over side edges of album; glue in place. Fold long edges of fabric over top and bottom edges of album, trimming fabric to fit approximately $1/4$" under album hardware; glue in place.
3. Cut two 2" x 9" strips of fabric. Press ends of each strip $1/4$" to wrong side. On inside of album, center and glue one strip along each side of album hardware with one long edge of each strip tucked $1/4$" under hardware.
4. Cut two $7^1/4$" x $8^3/4$" pieces of poster board and two $8^1/4$" x $9^3/4$" pieces of

fabric. Center one poster board piece on wrong side of one fabric piece. Fold corners of fabric diagonally over corners of poster board; glue in place. Fold remaining fabric edges over edges of poster board; glue in place. Repeat to cover remaining poster board piece.
5. Center and glue wrong side of poster board pieces inside front and back of album.
6. Cut a $4^3/4$" x $5^7/8$" piece of label fabric and a $4^1/2$" x $5^5/8$" piece of web. Center and fuse web to wrong side of label. Fringe edges of label to edges of web.
7. Trace "Family Recipes" pattern, page 106, onto tracing paper. Use transfer paper to transfer design to center of label. Use marker to draw over letters and to add "stitches" along edges of label. Center and fuse label on front of album.
8. Cut a 12" length of ribbon; tie ribbon into a bow. Glue bow to one corner of label and one button at each remaining corner.

RECIPE CARDS
You will need kitchen-motif fabric, paper-backed fusible web, 4" x 6" index cards, and 1"w satin ribbon.

1. Fuse web to wrong side of kitchen-motif fabric. Cut desired motifs from fabric. Fuse one motif to corner of each card.
2. Cut a 21" length of ribbon. Tie ribbon into a bow around cards.

GIFT JAR
You will need a canning jar, batting, poster board, and a scrap of kitchen-motif fabric.

1. Follow *Jar Lid Finishing*, page 121, to cover jar lid.

EASY MUSTARD PICKLES

*F*or those with a taste
for tangy foods, Easy Mustard
Pickles are a perfectly piquant
gift! Made in just a few easy steps,
our mouth-puckering sensations
are fantastic partners to holiday
foods. Pack the jar in an elf-face
bag that's created in a snap from
a white paper sack, a sock, and
scraps of craft foam and felt.

EASY MUSTARD PICKLES

1	quart whole sour dill pickles, drained and cut into $1/2$-inch slices
1	cup frozen chopped onions, thawed and drained
1	cup frozen chopped green pepper, thawed and drained
1	cup water
$1/4$	cup all-purpose flour
1	cup white vinegar
$1/3$	cup sugar
2	teaspoons dry mustard
$1^1/2$	teaspoons salt
1	teaspoon ground turmeric
1	teaspoon celery seed
1	teaspoon mustard seed

In a large bowl, combine pickles, onions, and green pepper. In a medium non-aluminum saucepan, gradually whisk water into flour until mixture is smooth. Whisk in vinegar, sugar, dry mustard, salt, turmeric, celery seed, and mustard seed. Whisking frequently, bring mixture to a boil over medium-high heat. Pour hot mixture over pickles; stir until well coated. Spoon mixture into heat-resistant jars with lids. Store in refrigerator.

Yield: about 5 cups pickles

ELF BAG

You will need tracing paper, peach and red craft foam, two black $1/2$" dia. buttons for eyes, glue, black permanent medium-point marker, lunch-size white paper bag, $3/4$" dia. white pom-pom, adult-size green sock, and $2^1/2$" of curly doll hair.

1. Trace ear and nose patterns, page 106, onto tracing paper. Use patterns to cut nose from red foam and ears from peach foam.
2. Glue nose and buttons on front of bag. Use marker to draw mouth on bag and detail line on ears.

3. Place gift in bag. Fold top of bag 1" to wrong side. Fold top corners diagonally to back of bag; glue to secure.
4. For hat, glue pom-pom to toe end of sock. Fold top of sock 2" to right side for cuff. Place hat on top of bag. Glue one ear in each pleat at sides of bag.
5. Glue one end of doll hair under cuff of hat; fringe opposite end.

OLIVE SPREAD TO GO

*B*ecause everyone's on the go, the holiday season is the ideal time to give quick-to-fix snacks. Nutty Olive Spread served on crackers is a true palate-pleaser. Share jars of this creamy, crunchy creation in hand-painted canvas totes tied with bows, and be sure to include crackers for munching.

NUTTY OLIVE SPREAD

>   2   packages (3 ounces each) cream cheese, softened
> 1/2   cup mayonnaise
>   1   jar (5³/₄ ounces) stuffed green olives, drained and finely chopped
> 1/2   cup finely chopped pecans, toasted
> 1/8   teaspoon ground black pepper
>   Crackers to serve

In a medium bowl, beat cream cheese until fluffy. Beat in mayonnaise. Stir in olives, pecans, and pepper. Cover and chill overnight to let flavors blend. Serve with crackers.

Yield: about 2 cups spread

CHRISTMAS MINI TOTES

For each tote, you will need red and green acrylic paint, paintbrushes, small canvas tote, gold paint pen, one 26" length each of 2"w red and red with gold stars sheer ribbon.

1. For each tote, use red and green paint to paint desired designs on front of tote. Use paint pen to add details to designs.
2. Tie ribbons into a bow around handles.

MICROWAVE MARMALADE

*I*n no time at all, you can
mix up a batch of Quick
Cranberry-Orange Jam using
your microwave! Just blend
orange marmalade with fresh
chopped cranberries to make
an ideal last-minute gift. For
a breakfast treat, pack a jar
of the concoction in a fabric-
lined wire basket along with
freshly baked biscuits for serving.

QUICK CRANBERRY-ORANGE JAM

  2 jars (18 ounces each) orange
       marmalade
  1 package (12 ounces) fresh
       cranberries, coarsely chopped

In a medium microwave-safe bowl,
combine marmalade and cranberries.
Cover and microwave on medium-high
power (80%) 6 minutes or until
marmalade melts and cranberries are
tender, stirring frequently. Spoon jam into
heat-resistant jars; cover and cool to
room temperature. Store in refrigerator.

Yield: about 4 cups jam

BERRY-TRIMMED BASKET

You will need a basket (we used a
7" x 9" wire basket), holly berry garland,
glue, fabric for basket liner, jar with lid,
string, and a button.
For tag, you will *also* need one
2¹/2" x 3³/4" piece each of paper-backed
fusible web and fabric, pinking shears,
green paper, black permanent fine-point
marker, and a 1¹/2" x 2³/4" white
paper piece.

1. Measure around rim of basket. Cut
a length of garland the determined
measurement; glue to basket.
2. Follow *Making a Basket Liner*,
page 123, to make liner with an
unfinished edge. Place liner in basket.
3. Measure around jar lid; add 7". Cut
two lengths of string the determined
measurement. Knot string around lid.
Glue button to knot.

4. For tag backing, fuse web to wrong side
of fabric; use pinking shears to trim
edges. Fuse fabric to green paper. Leaving
a ¹/4" green border, cut out tag backing.
Use marker to write "cranberry-orange
jam" on white paper piece. Center and
glue white paper piece to tag backing.

PLAYTIME SNACK MIX

*W*hen kids are on the move, feed them handfuls of our crunchy Playtime Snack Mix. The lively assortment is chock-full of bite-size peanut butter sandwich crackers for energy and multicolor candies for fun. These munchies are perfect for mile-a-minute young ones — especially when toted in a toy truck or purse!

PLAYTIME SNACK MIX

    1   package (10½ ounces) small
            peanut butter sandwich crackers
    ½   cup butter or margarine
    ½   cup firmly packed brown sugar
    1   cup (about 6 ounces) fruit-flavored
            building block-shaped candies
            (available at candy stores)
    ½   cup (about 4 ounces) small red
            gourmet jelly beans
    ½   cup (about 4 ounces) small green
            gourmet jelly beans

Preheat oven to 350 degrees. Place crackers in a single layer in a greased 10½ x 15½-inch jellyroll pan. In a heavy small saucepan, combine butter and brown sugar. Stirring constantly, cook over medium heat until sugar dissolves and mixture begins to boil. Without stirring, boil 3 minutes. Pour syrup over crackers, spreading syrup to coat crackers. Bake 5 to 7 minutes. Cool in pan.

Break crackers apart. In a large bowl, combine crackers, candies, and jelly beans. Store in an airtight container.

Yield: about 7 cups snack mix

SPICY COOKIE MIX

The aromas and flavors of spices naturally accompany the holidays, and desserts are no exception! Chocolate-Orange-Spice Cookie Mix is a sweet shortcut for busy folks. Give the easy-to-make mix in a plaid flannel bag accented with a felt reindeer and cookie cutter to make their baking festive.

CHOCOLATE-ORANGE-SPICE COOKIE MIX

8	cups all-purpose flour
2$\frac{1}{2}$	cups granulated sugar
2$\frac{1}{2}$	cups firmly packed brown sugar
1	cup cocoa
1	tablespoon dried orange peel
2	teaspoons ground cinnamon
2	teaspoons ground ginger
1$\frac{1}{2}$	teaspoons baking soda
1	teaspoon salt
2$\frac{3}{4}$	cups chilled butter or margarine, cut into pieces

In a very large bowl, combine flour, sugars, cocoa, orange peel, cinnamon, ginger, baking soda, and salt. Using a pastry blender or 2 knives, cut in butter until mixture resembles coarse meal. Divide mix evenly into 4 resealable plastic bags (about 4$\frac{1}{2}$ to 5 cups mix per bag). Store in refrigerator. Give with baking instructions.

Yield: about 18 cups cookie mix

To bake: Bring cookie mix to room temperature before mixing. Preheat oven to 375 degrees. In a medium bowl, combine cookie mix, 1 egg, 2 tablespoons milk, and 2 teaspoons vanilla extract; beat with an electric mixer until a soft dough forms. Divide dough in half. On a heavily floured surface, use a floured rolling pin to roll out half of dough to slightly less than $\frac{1}{8}$-inch thickness. Use a 4-inch-wide x 3$\frac{1}{2}$-inch-high reindeer-shaped cookie cutter to cut out cookies. Transfer to a lightly greased baking sheet. Bake 4 to 6 minutes or until bottoms are lightly browned. Transfer cookies to a wire rack to cool. Repeat with remaining dough. Store in an airtight container.

Yield: about 5 dozen cookies

FLANNEL GIFT BAG

You will need a 10$\frac{1}{2}$" x 25" piece of plaid flannel fabric, 3$\frac{1}{2}$" x 4" reindeer cookie cutter, 5" square white felt, glue, 23" length each of two coordinating colors of $\frac{1}{4}$"w grosgrain ribbon, one 6" length and two 23" lengths of jute twine, artificial greenery (we used a stem of holly leaves with berries), and two 1" dia. jingle bells.

1. Matching right sides and short edges, fold fabric in half. Using a $\frac{1}{4}$" seam allowance, sew sides of bag together. Turn bag right side out. Fringe top edge of bag.
2. Draw around cookie cutter on felt; cut out shape. Glue shape to bag front.
3. Place a bag of cookie mix in gift bag.
4. Tie ribbons and 23" lengths of jute into a bow around top of bag. Insert greenery into knot of bow; glue to secure.
5. Thread two jute streamers through shank of one jingle bell; knot ends together. Repeat for remaining bell and streamers.
6. Thread remaining length of jute through cookie cutter; tie to bag.

COOKIE MIX IN A JAR

*F*or a truly unique gift, we layered the ingredients for our old-fashioned cookies in a glass jar! A cross-stitched skirt for the lid adds holiday charm to this eye-catching offering. Be sure to include the baking instructions so that your pals can mix up a fresh batch of these delightfully sweet snacks.

OATMEAL-RAISIN COOKIE MIX

1¼ cups all-purpose flour
½ teaspoon baking powder
¼ teaspoon salt
1 cup quick-cooking oats
1 cup raisins
½ cup flaked coconut
½ cup firmly packed brown sugar
½ cup granulated sugar

In a small bowl, combine flour, baking powder, and salt; stir until well blended. Spoon flour mixture into a wide-mouth 1-quart jar with lid. Layer oats, raisins, coconut, brown sugar, and granulated sugar into jar. Cover with lid. Give with baking instructions.

Yield: about 4 cups cookie mix

To bake: Preheat oven to 350 degrees. Pour cookie mix into a large bowl and stir until ingredients are well blended. In a small bowl, combine ⅓ cup vegetable oil and 2 eggs; beat until blended. Add oil mixture to dry ingredients; stir until a soft dough forms. Drop teaspoonfuls of dough 2 inches apart onto a greased baking sheet or shape dough into 1-inch balls and roll in granulated sugar. Place balls 2 inches apart on a greased baking sheet; flatten with bottom of a glass dipped in granulated sugar. Bake 8 to 10 minutes or until bottoms are lightly browned. Transfer to a wire rack to cool. Store in an airtight container.

Yield: about 4 dozen cookies

CROSS STITCH JAR LID

You will need embroidery floss (see color key, page 106), a 7" square of White Aida (16 ct), 1-quart canning jar with a 3¼" dia. lid, batting, fabric for jar lid skirt, 21" length of lace trim, and a 24" length of ³/₈"w satin ribbon.

Refer to Cross Stitch and Embroidery Stitches, page 123, before beginning project.

1. Using two strands of floss for *Cross Stitch* and one strand for *Backstitch* and *French Knots*, center and stitch jar lid design, page 106, on Aida.
2. Use flat part of jar lid as a pattern and cut design from Aida and one circle from batting.
3. For jar lid skirt, draw around lid on wrong side of fabric. Cut out circle 2" outside drawn line. Center batting, then stitched piece on right side of skirt; pin in place. Stitching through all layers and covering raw edge of stitched piece, use a zigzag stitch to sew stitched piece to skirt.
4. Overlapping ends, use a zigzag stitch to sew trim along outer edge of skirt.
5. Center skirt over jar and replace band to secure.

FESTIVE CHERRY POPCORN BALLS

Speckled with the colors of Christmas and the yummy flavor of candied cherries, our popcorn balls are chewy, gooey, and delicious! Melted marshmallows are the "glue" that holds the popcorn and cherry bits together. A market basket trimmed with a ready-made prairie-point border and lined with cheery checked fabric makes it easy to carry the treats to one and all.

CANDIED CHERRY POPCORN BALLS

16 cups popped popcorn
1 package (4 ounces) red candied cherries, chopped
1 package (4 ounces) green candied cherries, chopped
$^1/_2$ cup butter or margarine
1 package (10$^1/_2$ ounces) miniature marshmallows
1 teaspoon almond extract

In a lightly greased large roasting pan, combine popcorn and cherries. Gently toss to mix. In a large saucepan, melt butter and marshmallows over medium-low heat. Remove from heat; stir in almond extract. Pour over popcorn mixture; stir to coat well. Use greased hands to firmly press mixture into about 2$^1/_2$-inch-diameter balls. Wrap individually in waxed paper.

Yield: about 1$^1/_2$ dozen popcorn balls

PRAIRIE BASKET

You will need a 1$^7/_8$" x 45" strip of muslin, glue, two 45" lengths of piping, 45" length of prairie-point edging, 8$^3/_4$" x 15" market basket with handle, artificial greenery (we used holly leaves with berries), several lengths of natural raffia, and a 24" x 30" torn fabric piece for basket liner.

1. For prairie-point trim, press raw edges of muslin strip $^1/_4$" to wrong side. Gluing raw edge of piping to wrong side, glue one piping length along one long pressed edge of muslin strip. Repeat for opposite edge.
2. Glue prairie-point edging along one long edge on wrong side of trim with points extending below piping.
3. Glue trim around rim of basket, overlapping ends as necessary.
4. Arrange and glue greenery on right side of trim.
5. Tie several lengths of raffia into a bow around handle.
6. Place liner in basket.

To give others a fast and nutritious start to the day, bundle a bag of our pancake mix in a "heart-y" basket tied with a bow, greenery, and snow-frosted pinecones. With a drizzling of sweet maple syrup, these breakfast delights will provide a burst of morning energy!

HEARTY PANCAKE MIX

- 1 cup old-fashioned oats
- 2 cups all-purpose flour
- 1½ cups whole-wheat flour
- 1 cup dry buttermilk powder
- ⅓ cup sugar
- 3 tablespoons baking powder
- 1 tablespoon baking soda
- 1 teaspoon dried orange peel
- 1 cup raisins
- 1 cup sliced almonds, toasted

Process oats in a food processor until coarsely ground. Add flours, buttermilk powder, sugar, baking powder, baking soda, and orange peel; process until blended. Transfer dry ingredients to a large bowl. Stir in raisins and almonds. Divide into 2 resealable plastic bags. Give with serving instructions.

Yield: about 6¼ cups pancake mix

To serve: Grease and preheat griddle. Combine 1 bag pancake mix, 1⅔ cups water, 1 egg, and 3 tablespoons vegetable oil in a medium bowl. Stir just until moistened. For each pancake, pour about ¼ cup batter onto griddle. Cook until top of pancake has a few bubbles and bottom is golden brown. Turn with a spatula and cook until remaining side is golden brown. Serve warm pancakes with syrup.

Yield: about 18 pancakes

HEART BASKET

You will need a heart-shaped basket with handle, paper-backed fusible web, fabric, poster board, glue, 1⅜ yds. of 1⅜"w wired ribbon, floral wire, wire cutters, and artificial greenery (we used pine stems with pinecones and a sprig of holly leaves).

For gift tag, you will *also* need colored pencils; photocopy of tag design (page 113); black permanent medium-point marker; one 2¾" x 4⅜" piece each of fabric, paper-backed fusible web, and poster board; hole punch; and a 6" length of black yarn.

1. Draw around heart side of basket on paper side of web. Fuse web to wrong side of fabric. Cut out along drawn line. Fuse fabric piece to poster board; cut out. Trim shape to fit inside edges of basket. Glue shape to basket.
2. Follow *Making a Bow*, page 121, to make a bow with four 7" loops, one 10" streamer, and one 6" streamer. Glue greenery and bow to handle.
3. Place pancake mix in plastic bag. Tie a length of ribbon into a bow around top of bag.
4. For gift tag, use colored pencils to color tag design; cut out. Use marker to write "Hearty Pancake Mix" and to add detail lines along inside edges of tag. Fuse web piece to wrong side of fabric piece; fuse fabric piece to poster board piece. Center and glue tag on fabric covered poster board. Punch hole in corner of tag. Thread yarn though hole and tie around gathers of bag.

ZIPPY CRANBERRY SALSA

*A*dd some zip to the same old chips and dip with our Cranberry Salsa. It's the perfect candidate for just such a snacking addiction, and it can also pep up meats! Ideal for the holidays, this tart and tangy blend is fun to give in a basket embellished with holiday greenery, ribbon, and a rustic cardboard star.

CRANBERRY SALSA

- 1 package (12 ounces) fresh cranberries, chopped
- 1 can (8 ounces) crushed pineapple in juice, drained
- $2/3$ cup sugar
- $1/2$ cup finely chopped green pepper
- $1/4$ cup chopped fresh cilantro
- 2 tablespoons finely chopped onion
- 1 jalapeño pepper, seeded and finely chopped
- $1/4$ teaspoon salt

In a large bowl, combine cranberries, pineapple, sugar, green pepper, cilantro, onion, jalapeño pepper, and salt. Cover and chill 2 hours to let flavors blend. Serve with chips or your favorite meat.

Yield: about 3 cups salsa

DECORATED MINI BASKET

You will need a basket with handle (we used a 7" dia. basket), $5/8$"w wired ribbon, glue, artificial greenery (we used pine stems and berries), tracing paper, corrugated cardboard, red paper, and a jar with $2^3/8$" dia. lid.

1. Measure around basket; add $1/2$". Cut a length of ribbon the determined

measurement. Overlapping ends at back, glue ribbon around rim of basket.

2. Cut a 15" length of ribbon. Tie ribbon into a bow around handle. Cut a sprig from greenery; glue to knot of bow.

3. Trace star patterns, page 108, separately onto tracing paper; cut out. Use patterns to cut one small star and one large star from cardboard. Leaving $1/2$" between shapes, glue stars to red paper. Leaving a $1/8$" red border, cut out each star.

4. Glue small star to knot of bow. Glue large star to top of jar lid.

5. Cut a small sprig from greenery; glue to star on jar lid.

ELF ENERGY SNACKS

*S*anta's little helpers make it simple to serve up batches of energy-packed Elf Snack Mix to friends and family during the holiday rush! Large metal cans are covered with construction paper for clever containers, and colored elf labels with a personal message provide a fun finish.

ELF SNACK MIX

2 packages (10 ounces each) miniature peanut butter sandwich cookies

2 packages (6 ounces each) sweetened dried cranberries

1 package (16 ounces) red and green candy-coated chocolate pieces

2 packages (10 ounces each) buttery toffee popcorn with peanuts

In a large container, combine cookies, dried cranberries, chocolate pieces, and popcorn mixture. Store in an airtight container.

Yield: about 22 cups snack mix

BUSY ELF CANS

For each can, you will need desired size can, colored paper, glue, tracing paper, transfer paper, bristol board, and colored pencils.

For small gift tag, you will *also* need a black permanent medium-point marker, 1⁷/₈" x 3¹/₈" piece of white paper, and a 2¹/₈" x 3³/₈" piece of colored paper.

For large gift tag, you will *also* need a black permanent medium-point marker,

2" x 3³/₈" piece of white paper, and a 2³/₈" x 3³/₄" piece of colored paper.

1. Measure around can; add ¹/₂". Measure height of can. Cut a piece from colored paper the determined measurements. Overlapping ends at back, glue paper around can.

2. Trace elf pattern, page 108, onto tracing paper. Use transfer paper to transfer design onto bristol board. Use colored pencils to color elf. Carefully cutting around elf's thumb, cut out elf.

3. For small or large gift tag, use marker to write message on white paper piece. Center and glue white paper piece to colored paper piece.

4. Inserting tag under elf's thumb, glue tag to elf. Glue elf to can.

MUFFIN BASKET

*S*livered almonds add nutty taste and crunchy texture to yummy Almond Muffins. They're great for snacking while opening gifts on Christmas morning, or you can bundle them up in a basket topped with a fabric-covered lid decorated with a charming winter scene. What better way to share these wholesome treats with others!

ALMOND MUFFINS

1$\frac{1}{3}$ cups all-purpose flour
$\frac{1}{2}$ cup firmly packed brown sugar
1 teaspoon baking powder
$\frac{1}{2}$ teaspoon baking soda
$\frac{1}{4}$ teaspoon salt
1 cup plus 2 tablespoons chopped sliced almonds, toasted and divided
$\frac{1}{2}$ cup buttermilk
$\frac{1}{4}$ cup butter or margarine, melted
2 eggs, beaten
$\frac{1}{2}$ teaspoon vanilla extract
$\frac{1}{2}$ teaspoon almond extract

Preheat oven to 350 degrees. In a medium bowl, combine flour, brown sugar, baking powder, baking soda, and salt. Stir in 1 cup almonds. Make a well in center of mixture. In a small bowl, combine buttermilk, melted butter, eggs, and extracts. Add to dry ingredients; stir just until moistened. Spoon batter into paper-lined muffin cups, filling each about one-half full. Sprinkle remaining 2 tablespoons almonds over muffins. Bake 20 to 25 minutes or until lightly browned and a toothpick inserted in center of muffin comes out clean. Remove from pan. Serve warm or cool on a wire rack. Store in an airtight container.

Yield: about 1 dozen muffins

PADDED BASKET LID

You will need a round basket (we used a 10" dia. basket), tracing paper, foam core board, craft knife, white fabric for lid lining, spray adhesive, batting, blue snow print fabric to cover lid, glue, assorted felt scraps, 1$\frac{1}{2}$" dia. wooden ball knob with hardware, white acrylic paint, paintbrush, and a nail.

1. For lid pattern, place basket upside down on tracing paper; draw around basket. Cut out circle along drawn line.
2. Spacing circles at least 2" apart, draw around pattern twice on foam core board.
3. Cutting along drawn line, use craft knife to cut one circle from foam core board. Trim circle to fit just inside basket rim.
4. Draw around pattern on wrong side of lining fabric. Cut out fabric circle 1$\frac{1}{2}$" outside drawn line. Clip curves to $\frac{1}{2}$" from drawn line. Apply spray adhesive to wrong side of fabric circle. Center foam circle on wrong side of fabric circle. Fold and glue edges of fabric to back of circle.
5. Cutting $\frac{3}{4}$" outside drawn line, cut out remaining foam core circle. Draw around circle on batting; cut out along drawn line. Apply spray adhesive to one side of batting. Center and glue batting circle to foam circle. Working with batting side down, repeat Step 4 to cover circle with snow print fabric.
6. Matching wrong sides and centering small circle on large circle, glue circles together.
7. Trace winter scene patterns, page 107, separately onto tracing paper. Use patterns to cut desired number of shapes from felt. Arrange shapes on top of lid; glue in place.
8. Paint knob as desired; allow to dry.
9. Use nail to punch a hole through center of lid. Attach knob to lid.

TOFFEE WAGON

Give a bundle of delectable Coffee Bean Toffee to a good neighbor this Christmas. Topped with a layer of melted chocolate chips, this java-flavored candy is sure to please a gourmet palate! Carry your homemade offering in a cute white wagon displaying a handmade gift tag.

COFFEE BEAN TOFFEE

     1   tablespoon instant coffee granules
    1/3 cup hot water
     1   cup butter
     1   cup sugar
     1   tablespoon light corn syrup
    1 1/2 cups slivered almonds, toasted
           and coarsely ground
    1/2 cup coarsely chopped chocolate-
           almond coffee beans
     1   teaspoon vanilla extract
    1/2 cup semisweet chocolate mini chips

Line a baking sheet with aluminum foil; grease foil. In a small bowl, dissolve coffee granules in hot water. Butter sides of a very heavy large saucepan. Combine butter, sugar, corn syrup, and coffee. Stirring constantly, cook over medium-low heat until sugar dissolves. Using a pastry brush dipped in hot water, wash down any sugar crystals on sides of pan. Attach a candy thermometer to pan, making sure thermometer does not touch bottom of pan. Increase heat to medium and bring to a boil. Cook, without stirring, until thermometer reaches hard-crack stage (approximately 300 to 310 degrees). Test about 1/2 teaspoon mixture in ice water. Mixture will form brittle threads in ice water and will remain brittle when removed from the water. Remove from heat and stir in almonds, coffee beans, and vanilla. Spread mixture onto prepared baking sheet. Sprinkle chocolate chips over hot candy; spread melted chocolate with a knife. Chill candy 1 hour or until chocolate hardens.

Break into pieces. Store in an airtight container between layers of waxed paper in a cool place.

Yield: about 1 pound, 10 ounces candy

HANDMADE GIFT TAG

You will need colored pencils, photocopy of tag design (page 113), red permanent fine-point marker, glue, and red paper.

1. Use pencils to color tag design. Use marker to write message on tag. Cut out tag.
2. Glue tag to red paper. Leaving a 1/4" red border, cut out gift tag.

REFRESHING CHOCOLATE MINTS

*A*nyone with a sweet tooth will be thankful for your offering of Peppermint Chocolate Creams! The luscious chocolate-covered mints provide a cool contrast to all the spicy foods of the holiday season. For a regal gift, package these refreshing candies in a pretty tin tied with Christmas ribbon and add a festive gift tag.

PEPPERMINT CHOCOLATE CREAMS

  1 jar (7 ounces) marshmallow creme
$^2/_3$ cup butter or margarine, softened
  1 teaspoon vanilla extract
$^3/_4$ teaspoon peppermint extract
  6 cups sifted confectioners sugar
  8 ounces chocolate candy coating, chopped
  1 candy bar (7 ounces) dark sweet chocolate, chopped

In a large bowl, beat marshmallow creme, butter, and extracts until well blended. Gradually add confectioners sugar, stirring until mixture is well blended. Shape teaspoonfuls of candy into $^3/_4$-inch balls. Place on a baking sheet lined with waxed paper. Chill 1 hour or until firm.

In top of a double boiler, melt candy coating and candy bar over hot, not simmering, water. Dip each candy into chocolate. Return to baking sheet lined with waxed paper. Chill until chocolate hardens. Store in an airtight container in a cool place.

Yield: about 9 dozen candies

HOLIDAY GIFT TAG

You will need red and green colored pencils, photocopy of tag design (page 113), red permanent fine-point marker, glue, and green paper.

1. Use pencils to color tag design. Use marker to write message on tag. Cut out tag.
2. Glue tag to green paper. Leaving a $^1/_8$" green border, cut out tag.

RED VELVET CUPCAKES

*W*hen the colorful batter is baked, our Red Velvet Cupcakes take on a crimson hue and a velvety texture. Topped with smooth cream cheese icing and packed in a ribbon-tied cupcake container, these delectable confections will make a special someone's day.

RED VELVET CUPCAKES

CAKE

- $^2/_3$ cup butter or margarine, softened
- $1^2/_3$ cups sugar
- 2 eggs, separated
- 1 bottle (1 ounce) red liquid food coloring
- 2 tablespoons vanilla extract
- $2^1/_4$ cups sifted cake flour
- $^1/_4$ cup cocoa
- 1 teaspoon baking soda
- $^3/_4$ teaspoon salt
- 1 cup plus 2 tablespoons buttermilk
- 2 teaspoons white vinegar

ICING

- 4 ounces cream cheese, softened
- $^1/_3$ cup vegetable shortening
- $^1/_3$ cup butter or margarine, softened
- $1^1/_2$ teaspoons clear vanilla extract
- $5^1/_3$ cups sifted confectioners sugar
- 1 tablespoon water
  Crushed red and green peppermint candies to decorate

Preheat oven to 350 degrees. For cake, cream butter and sugar in a large bowl until fluffy. Add egg yolks, food coloring, and vanilla; beat until smooth. In a medium bowl, combine cake flour, cocoa, baking soda, and salt. In a small bowl, combine buttermilk and vinegar.

Alternately beat dry ingredients and buttermilk mixture into creamed mixture, beating until well blended. Beat egg whites in a small bowl until stiff peaks form; fold into batter. Fill paper-lined muffin cups about two-thirds full. Bake 15 to 17 minutes or until a toothpick inserted in center of cupcake comes out clean. Transfer cupcakes to a wire rack to cool.

For icing, beat cream cheese, shortening, butter, and vanilla in a medium bowl until fluffy. Add confectioners sugar and water; beat until smooth. Ice each cupcake with about 1 tablespoon icing. Sprinkle candies on cupcakes. Store in an airtight container.

Yield: about $2^1/_2$ dozen cupcakes

MINTY CHOCOLATE COOKIES

*C*hocoholics will agree — our Chocolate-Mint Sandwich Cookies are a dreamy treat! Rich chocolate coating covers icing-filled crackers to make the doubly sweet delights. Place the cookies inside a painted coffee can laced with old Christmas cards for a resourceful presentation.

CHOCOLATE-MINT SANDWICH COOKIES

1½ packages (12 ounces each) round butter-flavored crackers

1 container (16 ounces) chocolate ready-to-spread frosting

1 package (1 pound, 8 ounces) chocolate candy coating, chopped

2 packages (10 ounces each) mint chocolate chips

Place half of crackers (about 84 crackers) on waxed paper. Spoon frosting into a pastry bag fitted with a large round tip. Pipe about 1 teaspoon frosting onto each cracker. Place remaining crackers on top of frosting and press lightly. In a heavy large saucepan, melt candy coating and chocolate chips over low heat. Remove from heat. Dip each cracker sandwich into chocolate. Place on waxed paper and let chocolate harden. Store in an airtight container in a cool place.

Yield: about 7 dozen cookies

"RECYCLED" CARD CAN

You will need red and green spray paint, clean dry can with lid (we used a 6¾"h x 6" dia. can), assorted Christmas cards, hole punch, ⅛"w red satin ribbon, glue, 2½"w red and white stripe wired ribbon, floral wire, and wire cutters.

1. Spray paint outside of can green and top and sides of lid red.
2. Trim cards to fit side of can. Punch two holes in top and bottom edges of each card.

3. Measure around can; add 8". Cut two lengths of ⅛"w ribbon the determined measurement. Lace one ribbon length through holes at top of cards. Repeat for bottom of cards.
4. Spacing cards evenly around can, spot glue cards to can to secure; tie ribbon ends into a bow.
5. Use wired ribbon and follow *Making a Bow*, page 121, to make a bow to fit lid of can. Tie two lengths of ⅛"w ribbon into a bow around knot. Center and glue bow to top of lid.

To create cookies with a gourmet twist, bake our Chocolate-Amaretto Biscotti! These crispy toast-like confections have a delicate flavor and a serious crunch, and they're wonderful for dipping in coffee or cocoa. Snuggle the cookies in a holly-ringed basket, along with a pair of festive mugs, to help your friends indulge themselves during the holiday season.

CHOCOLATE-AMARETTO BISCOTTI

This biscotti keeps well for several days.

- 1/2 cup butter or margarine, softened
- 1 cup sugar
- 2 eggs
- 3 tablespoons amaretto
- 1/2 teaspoon almond extract
- 2 1/4 cups all-purpose flour
- 1/4 cup cocoa
- 1 teaspoon baking powder
- 1/2 teaspoon baking soda
- 1/4 teaspoon salt
- 1 cup sliced almonds, toasted

Preheat oven to 375 degrees. Grease and flour a baking sheet. In a large bowl, cream butter and sugar until fluffy. Add eggs, amaretto, and almond extract; beat until smooth. In a medium bowl, combine flour, cocoa, baking powder, baking soda, and salt. Add dry ingredients to creamed mixture; stir until a soft dough forms. Stir in almonds. Divide dough into thirds. Allow 3 inches between loaves on prepared baking sheet. Shape each piece of dough into a 2 x 9-inch loaf, flouring hands as necessary. Bake 20 to 24 minutes or until loaves are firm. Cool 10 minutes on baking sheet.

Cut loaves diagonally into 1/2-inch slices. Lay slices flat on an ungreased baking sheet. Bake 6 minutes; turn slices over and bake 6 minutes longer. Transfer cookies to a wire rack to cool. Store in a cookie tin.

Yield: about 4 dozen cookies

HOLIDAY GIFT BASKET

You will need a basket with handles (we used an 11" dia. basket), red spray paint, holly berry garland, glue, 1 3/8"w plaid wired ribbon, two 6" lengths of floral wire, 1"w decorative white ribbon, and a cellophane bag.

For gift tag, you will *also* need red and green permanent medium-point markers, photocopy of tag design (page 113), and green paper.

1. Spray paint basket red.
2. Measure around basket; add 1". Cut a length from garland the determined measurement. Overlapping ends at back, glue garland around rim of basket.
3. Using wired ribbon, follow *Making a Bow*, page 121, to make bow with four 5" loops and two 3 1/2" streamers. Repeat using decorative ribbon. Center and glue decorative ribbon bow to wired ribbon bow. Glue bows to basket handle.
4. Place biscotti in bag. Tie decorative ribbon into a bow around top of bag.
5. Cut two stems from remaining garland. Glue one stem each to knot of bows on bag and basket.
6. For gift tag, use markers to color tag design; cut out. Use red marker to write message on tag. Glue tag to green paper. Leaving a 1/4" green border, cut out gift tag.

MUSTARD PRETZEL MUNCHIES

*F*or a snack assortment with a new twist, simply combine small pretzels and cheesy crackers with bite-size bagel chips and then bake the mixture in a buttery mustard blend. A fun tag and torn-fabric bow adorn the clever gift bag that's decorated with a wrap-around strip of poster board and a fused-on fabric panel.

MUSTARD PRETZEL MIX

2   packages (10 ounces each) small
    pretzel twists
2   packages (6 ounces each) bite-
    size plain bagel chips
1   package (10 ounces) cheese snack
    crackers
1¼ cups butter or margarine, melted
1¼ cups prepared mustard
2   teaspoons dry mustard
1½ teaspoons garlic powder
¼   teaspoon ground red pepper

Preheat oven to 250 degrees. Place pretzels, bagel chips, and cheese crackers in a large roasting pan. In a medium bowl, combine melted butter, prepared mustard, dry mustard, garlic powder, and red pepper; whisk until blended. Pour over pretzel mixture; toss until well coated. Bake 1½ hours, stirring every 15 minutes. Spread on aluminum foil to cool. Store in an airtight container.

Yield: about 28 cups pretzel mix

FABRIC-TRIMMED BAG

You will need a lunch-size brown paper bag, poster board, wood-tone spray, fabric for trim, paper-backed fusible web, 28

black permanent fine-point marker, and a 2½" x 23" torn fabric strip for bow. *For label,* you will *also* need a 3" x 6" piece of kraft paper, a 2½" square of green paper, yellow-colored pencil, tracing paper, transfer paper, stapler, and glue.

1. Measure bag from top front to top back; subtract 2". Cut a piece of poster board 5" wide by the determined measurement. Spray poster board with wood-tone spray.
2. Draw around poster board on paper side of web. Fuse web to wrong side of fabric. Cutting along drawn line for short edges and ½" inside long edges, cut out fabric. Center and fuse fabric on poster board.

3. Use marker to draw "stitches" over edges of fabric.
4. Centering and matching one short end to top front of bag, wrap fused poster board around bag; glue in place.
5. Trace label pattern, page 109, onto tracing paper. Use transfer paper to transfer words to green paper piece. Color letters yellow. Use marker to outline letters and draw "stitches" along edges of green paper piece.
6. For card, match short edges and fold kraft paper piece in half. With fold at top, center and glue green paper piece to front of card. Glue card to front of bag.
7. Place gift in bag. Fold top of bag 2" to back; staple closed. Tie torn fabric strip into a bow and glue over staple.

HOMEY BRANDIED PEACHES

*S*erving dessert provides a wonderful opportunity to add a scrumptious finish to a well-planned meal. When the palate is ready to enjoy something sweet, spoon Brandied Peaches over slices of pound cake. For a lasting touch, send jars of the homemade concoction, packaged in quaint cottage bags, home with your guests.

BRANDIED PEACHES

> 2 cans (15¼ ounces each) sliced
> peaches in heavy syrup
> ½ cup peach brandy

Drain peaches, reserving 1 cup syrup. Spoon peaches into a 2-quart container with lid. In a small bowl, combine brandy and reserved syrup. Pour over peaches. Cover and store in refrigerator overnight to let flavors blend. Serve over pound cake or ice cream.

Yield: about 5 cups peaches

COTTAGE BAG

You will need paper-backed fusible web, assorted fabrics for appliqués, lunch-size brown paper bag, stapler, 1" dia. button, ½" dia. button, six ⅝" dia. buttons, and glue.

For gift tag, you will *also* need poster board, kraft paper, and a black permanent fine-point marker.

1. Follow *Making Appliqués*, page 122, to make one each of door frame 2½" x 4½", door 2" x 4¼", door window 1" x 1¾", window frame 2¼" x 2⅜", window 1⅞" x 2", chimney

1⅜" x 2⅜", and tree trunk ¼" x 3⅛" appliqués. Make one roof appliqué 3½" by width of bag.

2. Arrange all appliqués except chimney on front of bag, overlapping as necessary; fuse in place.

3. Place gift in bag.

4. Fold corners diagonally to back leaving 1" of center top of bag unfolded. Staple corners in place.

5. Glue 1" dia. button to window, ½" dia. button to door, and ⅝" dia. buttons along tree trunk.

6. For gift tag, fuse chimney to poster board; cut out. Cut a 1⅛" x 1⅝" piece from kraft paper. Use marker to write message on tag. Glue tag to chimney. Glue chimney to roof.

BASKET OF BRIE

*I*t's hard to believe
that such a simple recipe
makes an appetizer that
tastes this good! Brie
Dip is an irresistible gourmet
delicacy that you can share,
complete with ready-to-eat
breadsticks, in a gift basket
tied with a holiday bow.

BRIE DIP

8 ounces Brie cheese
1/4 cup finely chopped green onions
2 cloves garlic, minced
2 tablespoons vegetable oil
1 tablespoon Dijon mustard
1/8 teaspoon ground red pepper
1 cup mayonnaise
Purchased breadsticks to give

Remove rind from cheese; cut cheese
into several pieces. In a medium skillet,
sauté green onions and garlic in oil over
medium heat until tender. Reduce heat to
medium-low. Stirring constantly, add
cheese, mustard, and red pepper; stir
until cheese melts. Remove from heat and
stir in mayonnaise. Transfer to a
microwave-safe container. Cover and store
in refrigerator. Give with serving
instructions and breadsticks.

Yield: about 1³/4 cups dip

To serve: Cover and microwave on
medium power (50%) 5 minutes or until
softened, stirring every 2 minutes. Serve
with breadsticks.

DECORATED BASKET WITH BOW

You will need a basket with an open
weave around center (we used a white

7¹/₂" x 10¹/₂" oval basket), 1¹/₄"w wired
ribbon, floral wire, wire cutters, artificial
greenery (we used two sprigs of holly
leaves with berries), red shredded paper,
piece of clear cellophane (large enough
to wrap bowl), clear cellophane bag,
and two 19" lengths of ⁵/₈"w green
satin ribbon.

For gift tag, you will *also* need red and
green colored pencils, photocopy of tag
design (page 113), and a black
permanent medium-point marker.

1. Measure around basket; add 3". Cut a
length of wired ribbon the determined
measurement. Beginning and ending at
center front, weave ribbon around basket.

2. Use wired ribbon and follow *Making a
Bow,* page 121, to make a bow with six 6"
loops and two 4" streamers. Use wire at
back of bow to secure bow to basket over
ribbon ends. Glue greenery to center of
bow. Place shredded paper in basket.
3. Place bowl of dip at center of
cellophane. Gather cellophane over top of
bowl. Tie satin ribbon into a bow around
gathers. Place breadsticks in bag. Tie
remaining ribbon length around top of
bag; place bowl and bag in basket.
4. For gift tag, use pencils to color tag.
Use marker to write baking instructions
on tag. Glue tag to red paper. Leaving a
¹/₈" red border, cut out tag.

30

VOLCANO PIZZA PIE

*C*olossal in size
and chock-full of meats,
vegetables, and cheeses,
our Volcano Pizza Pie
satisfies enormous appetites!
Deliver the all-in-one meal
in a handy basket along with
plates, napkins, and utensils.
What a tasty way to share
warm Christmas wishes
with friends!

VOLCANO PIZZA PIE

    8 ounces Italian sausage
    1 cup chopped onion
    1 cup chopped green pepper
    1 can (2¹/₄ ounces) sliced black
       olives, well drained
  ¹/₂ cup sliced green olives, well
       drained
    1 jar (2¹/₂ ounces) sliced
       mushrooms, well drained
    1 can (10 ounces) refrigerated
       pizza crust dough
    1 package (8 ounces) shredded
       combined mozzarella and
       Cheddar cheese
    1 package (3¹/₂ ounces) pepperoni
       slices
 1¹/₂ cups diced Canadian bacon
       (about 8 ounces)
    1 cup prepared pizza sauce

In a medium skillet, brown sausage over medium-high heat. Reserving sausage drippings, transfer sausage to paper towels to drain; crumble. Add onion and green pepper to drippings in skillet; cook just until vegetables are tender. Transfer to paper towels to drain. Place olives and mushrooms on separate paper towels; pat dry.

Preheat oven to 425 degrees. Unroll pizza dough onto lightly floured plastic wrap. Use a floured rolling pin to roll dough into a 10-inch square. Using plastic wrap, transfer dough to a greased 9-inch aluminum foil cake pan. Reserve ³/₄ cup of cheese for top of pizza. Layer dough with half of pepperoni, onion mixture, mushrooms, Canadian bacon, olives, sausage, cheese, and pizza sauce. Repeat layers. Leaving a 1¹/₂-inch opening at top of pizza, pull corners of dough up over filling. Loosely cover with foil and bake 15 minutes on lowest rack of oven. Remove foil and bake 10 minutes longer. Sprinkle reserved cheese over center of pizza. Bake 5 more minutes or until cheese melts. Let pizza stand 15 minutes before serving. Serve warm.

Yield: about 8 servings

MULLED CIDER BASKET

Sitting in front of a blazing fire will be even more relaxing with cups of steaming mulled cider. Our easy-to-prepare spice mixture adds holiday zest to plain apple cider. Nestle the mull in a decorative basket next to a pair of aromatic mug mats for a welcome gift.

SPICED APPLE CIDER MULL

- 2 tablespoons loose tea leaves
- 4 teaspoons whole cloves
- 1 tablespoon whole allspice
- 2 cinnamon sticks, halved
- 1 cardamom pod, crushed
- 1 teaspoon dried orange peel
  Cinnamon sticks to give

In a small bowl, combine tea leaves, cloves, allspice, halved cinnamon sticks, cardamom pod, and dried orange peel. Transfer mix to a plastic bag. Store in a cool place. Give with serving instructions and cinnamon sticks.

Yield: about $1/3$ cup mull mix

To serve: Combine mull mix, 1 gallon apple cider, and $1/2$ cup granulated sugar in a large Dutch oven over medium heat; cover and bring to a simmer. Reduce heat and simmer 20 minutes. Strain and discard mull mix. Serve hot with cinnamon sticks.

Yield: about 16 cups mulled cider

SPICE MUG MATS IN GIFT BASKET

You will need artificial greenery to line basket and a basket with handle (we used an $8^1/2$" x 12" oval basket).

For gift bag, you will *also* need a $5^1/2$" x 14" piece of fabric, pinking shears, raffia, glue, two cinnamon sticks, dried apple slice, and an artificial greenery sprig (we used holly leaves with berries).

For each mug mat, you will *also* need paper-backed fusible web, fabric for appliqués and binding, two $5^1/2$" squares of fabric, and $1/8$ cup each of cloves and rice.

For gift tag, you will *also* need decorative-edge craft scissors, one piece each of tan and brown paper, brown and black permanent medium-point markers, hole punch, and a 12" length of jute twine.

1. Line basket with greenery.

2. Matching right sides and short edges, fold $5^1/2$" x 14" fabric piece in half. Using a $1/4$" seam allowance, sew sides of bag together. Use pinking shears to trim top of bag. Place a bag of cider mull in fabric bag. Tie raffia into a bow around top of bag. Glue cinnamon sticks, apple slice, and greenery sprig to bow.

3. For each mug mat, use patterns, page 109, and follow *Making Appliqués,* page 122, to make one each apple, stem, and leaf appliqués from fabrics.

4. Arrange appliqués on right side of one fabric square; fuse in place.

5. Cut four 1" x 6" binding strips from fabric. Press ends of each strip $1/4$" to wrong side. Press one long raw edge of each strip $1/4$" to wrong side.

6. Matching wrong sides, place fabric squares together. Matching raw edges, pin one binding strip to one side edge on appliquéd side of mat. Using a $1/4$" seam allowance, sew through all layers. Press binding over raw edges to back of mat; pin in place. Hand sew binding to back of mat.

7. Repeat to sew a second strip to opposite edge and a third strip to bottom of mat.

8. Repeat step 6 to sew remaining binding strip to top edge of mat. Fill mat with cloves and rice; sew opening closed.

9. For gift tag, use craft scissors to cut a 2" x $3^1/2$" piece from tan paper. Use markers to write message on tag. Glue tag to brown paper. Leaving a $1/4$" brown border, cut out tag. Punch hole in corner of tag. Thread twine through hole and around basket handle. Tie twine into a bow at front of tag.

SPIRITED BRANDY BALLS

*N*utty, flaky, or powdery — three kinds of coatings on our Brandied Date-Nut Balls make a delicious difference! These marvelous munchies will be welcome wherever friends gather during the holidays. To make a gift of the delightful candies, place them in an ornament-appliquéd tin.

BRANDIED DATE-NUT BALLS

    2   packages (8 ounces each)
            chopped dates
 1¹/₂   cups granulated sugar
    1   cup flaked coconut
 ¹/₃   cup brandy
    1   cup finely chopped pecans
 ¹/₂   cup flaked coconut, toasted
 ¹/₄   cup finely chopped pecans, toasted
 ¹/₄   cup confectioners sugar

In a large microwave-safe bowl, combine dates, granulated sugar, 1 cup coconut, and brandy. Cover and microwave on high power (100%) 8 minutes, stirring every 2 minutes. Stir in 1 cup pecans. When cool enough to handle, use greased hands to roll into 1-inch balls. Roll one-third of balls in toasted coconut, one-third of balls in toasted pecans, and one-third of balls in confectioners sugar. Store in an airtight container in a cool place.

Yield: about 5 dozen candies

APPLIQUÉD CANDY TIN

You will need red spray paint, candy tin with lid (we used an 8" dia. tin), batting, gold fabric to cover lid, paper-backed fusible web, red and green fabrics for

appliqués, tear-away stabilizer, thread to coordinate with appliqués, glue, twelve assorted buttons, green fabric for side trim, 12" length of ¹/₁₆"w green satin ribbon, and corrugated cardboard.

1. Spray paint outside of tin red.
2. Draw around lid on batting and wrong side of gold fabric. Cut out batting circle along drawn line and fabric circle ³/₈" outside drawn line.
3. Follow *Tracing Patterns*, page 121, to make ornament and band patterns, page 109. Follow *Making Appliqués*, page 122, to make four ornament appliqués from red fabric and four band appliqués from green fabric. Arrange appliqués at center on right side of fabric circle; fuse in place.
4. Follow *Machine Appliqué*, page 122, and use coordinating thread to stitch around appliqués. Glue three buttons along each band.
5. Glue batting circle to top of lid. Center and glue fabric circle over batting. Make

¹/₂" clips in fabric around lid. Glue edges to sides of lid. Trim edge of fabric just above bottom edge of lid if necessary.
6. Measure around lid; add ¹/₂". Cut a strip of fabric ⁷/₈" by the determined measurement. Press each edge of strip ¹/₄" to wrong side. Overlapping ends and covering edges of fabric, glue strip around side of lid.
7. Tie ribbon length into a bow; glue to center of lid.
8. For dividers, measure diameter of tin. Measure height of tin; subtract ¹/₄". Cut one long divider from cardboard the determined measurements. Cut one short divider from cardboard one-half the diameter measurement by the determined height measurement.
9. Mark center of long divider. Mark short divider ¹/₄" from one short end. Leaving ¹/₂" uncut, cut across each divider where marked.
10. Place long divider cut side up in center of tin. Place short divider cut side down over cut in long divider.

"DOGGONE" TASTY TREATS

*D*on't forget about
man's best friend at
Christmastime! A batch
of homemade dog biscuits
is a fun gift idea for families
with canine companions.
For a "doggone" cheery
presentation, pack the goodies
in a decorated dish, then
gather it in cellophane and
add a beribboned jingle bell.

BONE APPÉTIT TREATS

  1 cup whole-wheat flour
  $^1/_2$ cup all-purpose flour
  $^1/_2$ cup cornmeal
  $^1/_4$ cup nonfat dry milk powder
  $^1/_2$ teaspoon garlic powder
  $^1/_2$ cup vegetable oil
  $^1/_2$ cup beef or chicken broth

   Preheat oven to 300 degrees. In a medium bowl, combine flours, cornmeal, dry milk, and garlic powder. Add oil and broth; stir until well blended. On a lightly floured surface, use a floured rolling pin to roll out dough to $^1/_2$-inch thickness. Use a 5-inch-long bone-shaped cookie cutter to cut out treats. Transfer to a greased baking sheet. Bake 25 to 27 minutes or until firm and bottoms are lightly browned. Transfer treats to a wire rack to cool. Store in an airtight container in a cool place.

Yield: about 10 large dog treats

JINGLE DOG DISH

You will need tracing paper, white craft foam, black permanent medium-point marker, glue, pet food dish, clear cellophane, 28" length of 2$^1/_2$"w wired

ribbon, 12" length of $^1/_2$"w satin ribbon, and a 45mm jingle bell.

1. Trace bone pattern, page 109, onto tracing paper; cut out. Use pattern to cut bone from craft foam.
2. Use marker to write "Bone Appétit!" on bone. Glue bone to dish.

3. Fill dish with dog treats. Place dish at center of cellophane. Gather edges of cellophane over dish. Tie wired ribbon into a bow around gathers. Thread satin ribbon through shank of bell; tie ribbon around gathers.

TART-AND-TANGY JAM

*C*omplement fresh-baked breads with our delicious Cherry Christmas Jam. It's the perfect partner for biscuits, rolls, and more! Friends will love the homemade delicacy even more when it's delivered in cute jars accented with quilt-look lids.

CHERRY CHRISTMAS JAM

- 2 cans (14½ ounces each) pitted tart red cherries in water, drained
- 6 cups sugar
- ⅓ cup freshly squeezed lemon juice
- 2 pouches (3 ounces each) liquid fruit pectin
- 1 teaspoon almond extract
- ½ teaspoon red liquid food coloring

Process cherries in a food processor until coarsely chopped. In a heavy Dutch oven, combine cherries, sugar, and lemon juice. Stirring constantly over high heat, bring mixture to a rolling boil. Stir in liquid pectin. Stirring constantly, bring to a rolling boil again and boil 1 minute. Remove from heat; skim off foam. Stir in almond extract and food coloring. Spoon jam into heat-resistant jars; cover and cool to room temperature. Store in refrigerator.

Yield: about 6½ cups jam

DECORATED JAR LIDS

For each jar lid, you will need a canning jar with lid, cream-colored fabric, batting, cardboard, paper-backed fusible web, fabric scrap for appliqué, black permanent fine-point marker, glue, button, and several lengths of raffia.

For each gift bag, you will *also* need fabric for liner, gift bag with handles (large enough to accommodate jar), artificial greenery (we used a holly stem with berries).

1. For each jar lid insert, use flat part of jar lid as a pattern and cut one circle each from cream fabric, batting, and cardboard.
2. Use pattern, page 110, and follow *Making Appliqués*, page 122, to make one star appliqué from fabric scrap. Center star on fabric circle; fuse in place. Use marker to draw "stitches" around star.

3. Glue batting circle to cardboard circle. Center fabric circle right side up on batting; glue edges of fabric circle to batting. Glue button to center of star.
4. Before presenting gift, remove band from filled jar. Place jar lid insert in band and replace band on jar. Tie several lengths of raffia into a bow around band.
5. For bag liner, follow *Making a Basket Liner*, page 123, to make liner with an unfinished edge. Place liner, then jar in bag. Insert end of greenery into hole for handle in bag; glue to secure.

NUTTY MOCHA MIX

*H*ot cups of cocoa with a dash of nutty flavor — that's what you give your pals when you share Hazelnut Mocha Mix. Simply combine the dry ingredients and then fill fabric-adorned paper bags with the mix. Friends and family are sure to enjoy sipping your thoughtful winter warmer!

HAZELNUT MOCHA MIX

- 1 package (1 pound, 9.6 ounces) nonfat dry milk powder
- 1 package (16 ounces) confectioners sugar, sifted
- 1 package (15 ounces) chocolate mix for milk
- 1 jar (11 ounces) non-dairy powdered creamer
- 2 jars (8 ounces each) hazelnut-flavored non-dairy powdered creamer
- $1/2$ cup cocoa
- $1/4$ cup instant coffee granules

In a very large bowl, combine dry milk, confectioners sugar, chocolate mix, creamers, cocoa, and coffee granules; stir until well blended. Store in resealable plastic bags. Give with serving instructions.

Yield: about $18 1/4$ cups mocha mix

To serve: Pour 6 ounces hot water over 3 tablespoons mix; stir until well blended.

DECORATED BAGS

For each bag, you will need a black permanent fine-point marker, brown paper bottle bag, Christmas-motif fabric, glue, and a stapler.

1. Use marker to write "Hazelnut Mocha Mix" on front of bag. Cut one motif from fabric; glue to front of bag.
2. Place plastic bag of drink mix in bag. Fold top of bag 2" to front. Staple to secure.

3. Cut a piece of fabric 4" by width of bag. Using fabric design as a guide, trim one edge across width of fabric. Folding 1" of straight edge over to back, glue fabric piece to front of bag.

POWER POPCORN

*P*acking the natural energy of dried fruit and the sweetness of golden caramel popcorn, Candied Dried Fruit and Popcorn makes a super pick-me-up for the busiest season of the year. Let the appetizing tidbits peek through a cellophane-lined window in your jolly gift bag.

CANDIED DRIED FRUIT AND POPCORN

12	cups popped popcorn
1	cup sliced almonds
1½	cups firmly packed brown sugar
¾	cup butter or margarine
6	tablespoons light corn syrup
¾	teaspoon salt
1½	teaspoons vanilla extract
¾	teaspoon baking soda
1	cup dried blueberries
1	cup sweetened dried cranberries

Preheat oven to 200 degrees. Place popcorn and almonds in a greased large roasting pan. In a heavy medium saucepan, combine brown sugar, butter, corn syrup, and salt. Stirring constantly, cook over medium-low heat until sugar dissolves. Increase heat to medium and bring syrup to a boil. Cook, without stirring, 5 minutes. Remove from heat. Stir in vanilla and baking soda (mixture will foam). Stir in blueberries and cranberries. Stir syrup into popcorn mixture (may clump together). Bake 1¼ hours, stirring every 15 minutes. Spread on lightly greased aluminum foil to cool. Store in an airtight container.

Yield: about 18 cups popcorn

CHRISTMAS WINDOW BAG

You will need tracing paper, 8" x 10¼" gift bag, craft knife, cardboard to fit inside bag, clear cellophane, glue, kraft paper, serrated-edge craft scissors, black permanent fine-point marker, ⅞"w red and 1⅜"w green wired ribbon, 6" length of floral wire, and artificial greenery (we used pine stems, holly leaves, and berries).

For gift tag, you will *also* need colored pencils, photocopy of tag design (page 113), black permanent medium-point marker, red paper, and decorative-edge craft scissors.

1. For window pattern, draw a 4" x 5¼" rectangle on tracing paper; cut out. With one long edge of pattern 1⅜" from bottom of bag, center pattern side to side on front of bag. Draw around pattern.
2. Place cardboard in bag and use craft knife to cut along drawn line for window opening in bag.
3. Cut a piece of cellophane ⅜" larger on all sides than pattern. Center and glue cellophane over opening on inside of bag.
4. Draw around pattern on kraft paper. Use craft scissors to cut out window frame ⅜" inside and outside drawn line. Use marker to draw designs on border as desired. Center border over window; glue in place.
5. Centering red ribbon on green ribbon, follow *Making a Bow*, page 121, to make bow with six 8" loops and two 5½" streamers. Glue greenery to knot of bow. Glue bow to bag.
6. For gift tag, use pencils to color tag design; cut out. Use marker to write message on tag. Glue tag to red paper. Leaving a ⅛" red border, use craft scissors to cut out gift tag. Glue tag to bow.

QUICK-AS-A-WINK CANDY

*Y*ou can whip up a batch of Quick-As-A-Wink Candy faster than Santa comes down the chimney! Concocted in just a few minutes using the microwave, these chocolate and peanut butter mouthfuls boast an unbelievably sumptuous flavor. Ribbon-tied bags of the treats served up in plastic goblets make a simple but classy gift for anyone on your list.

QUICK-AS-A-WINK CANDY

   1 package (16 ounces) chocolate-
      covered vanilla cream drop
      candies
   1 cup crunchy peanut butter
2¹/₂ tablespoons butter or margarine

Place candies, peanut butter, and butter in a large microwave-safe bowl. Microwave on medium-high power (80%) 2 minutes or until candies melt and mixture is smooth, stirring after 1 minute. Drop by teaspoonfuls onto waxed paper. Let candy harden. Store in an airtight container in a cool place.

Yield: about 6 dozen candies

GIFT GOBLETS

For each gift, you will need a plastic stemmed goblet, cellophane bag to fit inside goblet, 14" length of ³/₈"w wired ribbon, glue, and artificial greenery (we used a sprig of holly leaves with berries). *For gift tag,* you will *also* need green and red colored pencils, photocopy of tag design (page 113), red permanent fine-point marker, red paper, serrated-edge

craft scissors, hole punch, and a 6" length of yarn.

1. Place bag in goblet; place candy in bag. Gather bag around top of candy. Tie ribbon into a bow around gathers. Glue holly sprig to knot of bow.

2. For gift tag, use pencils to color tag design. Cut out tag. Use marker to write message on tag. Glue tag to red paper. Leaving a ¹/₈" red border, use craft scissors to cut out gift tag. Punch hole in corner of tag. Thread yarn through hole and tie around gathers of bag.

40

"DE-LIGHT-FUL" DESSERT

*N*o one will believe
this treat is low in fat because
it tastes so sinfully rich! Light
Chocolate Eclair Dessert uses
low-fat and no-fat ingredients
that make it good for the figure
yet tasty, too! Indulge friends
with the delightful dessert
accompanied by a card
adorned with a string of
handmade "lights."

LIGHT CHOCOLATE ECLAIR DESSERT

- 2 packages (1 ounce each) white
  chocolate sugar-free instant
  pudding mix
- 3 cups skim milk
- 1 container (8 ounces) fat-free frozen
  whipped topping, thawed
- 42 low-fat graham crackers (2½-inch
  squares)
- 1 jar (16½ ounces) fat-free fudge
  topping
- 1 ounce white baking chocolate,
  melted

In a large bowl, add pudding mix to
milk; beat until thickened. Fold in
whipped topping. Place a layer of graham
crackers in bottom of an ungreased
x 13-inch baking dish. Spoon 3 cups
pudding over crackers. Repeat with
another layer of crackers and pudding.
Top with remaining crackers. Spread
fudge topping over crackers. Drizzle
melted white chocolate over topping.
Cover and chill overnight. Cut into 2-inch
squares.

Yield: 24 servings

1 serving (2-inch square): 186 calories,
1.0 gram fat, 2.5 grams protein,
26.9 grams carbohydrates

STRING-OF-LIGHTS GIFT CARD

You will need red and green paper, black
permanent fine-point marker, glue,
5" x 7" stationery card, spray adhesive,
gold mylar wrapping paper, poster board,
tracing paper, six 5" lengths of gold wired
cord, and two black chenille stems.

1. Cut a 2¾" x 4½" piece from red
paper. Use marker to write message
on paper piece; center and glue to
card front.
2. Apply spray adhesive to wrong side of
mylar; glue to poster board.
3. Trace pattern, page 109, onto tracing
paper; cut out. Draw around pattern six

times on poster board side of mylar and
three times each on red and green
papers. Cut out shapes.
4. Leaving socket portion of bulb
untrimmed, trim ⅛" from edges of red
and green bulbs.
5. Matching sockets, glue paper bulbs to
mylar bulbs.
6. Alternating red and green bulbs, use
marker to write one word each on bulbs:
"Light," "Chocolate," "Eclair," "Dessert,"
"Enjoy!," and "Yum!"
7. Tie each cord length into a bow; glue
one bow to each bulb.
8. For light string, twist chenille stems
together end to end to form circle.
Arrange light string around edge of
card; glue in place. Glue bulbs around
light string.

CHOCOLATE PRALINE SAUCE

*A*s tasty as the
old-fashioned candy,
Chocolate Praline Sauce
is just the thing to satisfy a
sweet tooth. The creamy,
nutty mixture transforms ice-
cream or pound cake into
unforgettable desserts! "Plant"
the gift in a flowerpot look-
alike made from a pint-size
ice-cream container.

CHOCOLATE PRALINE SAUCE

- 2 cups firmly packed brown sugar
- 1 cup dark corn syrup
- 1/2 cup butter or margarine
- 1 cup whipping cream
- 1 package (6 ounces) semisweet chocolate chips
- 1 1/2 teaspoons vanilla extract
- 2 cups chopped pecans, toasted

In a heavy medium saucepan, combine brown sugar, corn syrup, and butter. Stirring constantly, bring to a simmer over medium-low heat; cook 15 minutes or until sugar dissolves. Remove from heat. Whisk in whipping cream, chocolate chips, and vanilla; whisk until chocolate melts. Stir in pecans. Spoon sauce into pint jars; cover and store in refrigerator. Serve sauce warm or at room temperature over cake or ice cream.

Yield: about 5 cups sauce

ICE-CREAM CARTON FLOWERPOT

You will need a pint-size ice-cream container, spray primer, terra-cotta spray paint, green and red paint pens, black permanent fine-point marker, green

fabric, pinking shears, pint-size jar with 2 3/4" dia. lid, rubber band, and a 24" length of 1/2"w red satin ribbon.

Follow Painting Techniques, page 122, for painting tips. Allow primer and paint to dry after each application.

1. Spray paint container and lid with primer, then terra-cotta paint. Use paint pens and marker to draw designs on outside of container and lid.

2. Center and glue container on lid to resemble flowerpot.
3. Draw around jar lid on wrong side of fabric. Use pinking shears to cut out circle 2" outside drawn line. Center fabric circle over jar lid; secure with rubber band. Tie ribbon into a bow around lid, covering rubber band. Place jar in flowerpot.

GOOD-NEIGHBOR BREAD

*S*oft loaves of our
*Date-Nut Bread are perfect
for sharing with neighborhood
friends, and they're really easy
to make, too! For a woodsy
holiday look, deliver the nut-
filled loaves in novelty wooden
crates lined with fabric.*

DATE-NUT BREAD

  2 packages (8 ounces each)
      chopped dates
1¹/₄ cups apple juice
 ¹/₂ cup granulated sugar
 ¹/₂ cup firmly packed brown sugar
  1 egg
 ¹/₃ cup butter or margarine, melted
1¹/₂ teaspoons vanilla extract
2³/₄ cups all-purpose flour
1¹/₂ teaspoons baking powder
 ¹/₄ teaspoon salt
1¹/₂ cups chopped walnuts

Preheat oven to 325 degrees. Combine dates and apple juice in a medium microwave-safe bowl. Cover and microwave on high power (100%) 2 minutes or until juice is hot. Let mixture stand 5 minutes.

In a large bowl, beat sugars, egg, melted butter, and vanilla until smooth. Reserving dates, drain apple juice into sugar mixture; beat until well blended. In a medium bowl, combine flour, baking powder, and salt. Add dry ingredients to sugar mixture; beat just until blended. Stir in dates and walnuts. Spoon batter into 2 greased 4¹/₂ x 8¹/₂-inch loaf pans. Bake about 1 hour or until a toothpick inserted in center of bread comes out with a few crumbs clinging. Cool in pans on a wire rack 10 minutes. Transfer loaves to wire

rack to cool completely. Store in an airtight container.

Yield: 2 loaves bread

GIFT CRATE AND TAG

You will need fabric for liner and a wooden crate with handle (we used a 6" x 9¹/₂" crate with evergreen tree sides). *For gift tag,* you will *also* need two each 2" and 3¹/₂" twigs, 2" x 3¹/₂" piece of cream-colored heavy paper, hole punch, 34" length of jute twine, glue, artificial

greenery (we used a sprig of pine needles with a small pinecone), and a black permanent medium-point marker.

1. Follow *Making a Basket Liner,* page 123, to make liner for crate with an unfinished edge.
2. For gift tag, glue twigs along sides of paper piece. Use marker to write message on tag. Punch hole in corner of tag; thread jute through hole and tie into a bow around handle. Glue greenery to corner of tag.

ROBUST CHEESE SPREAD

*F*or the discerning
palate, present a robust
delicacy — our Port Wine
Cheese Spread. The tasty
blend of cheeses and wine
makes this spread a favorite
of family and friends. Deliver
the easy-to-fix cheese packed
in festive clay flowerpots
displayed in beribboned
baskets. Be sure to include
crackers to complete the gifts.

PORT WINE CHEESE SPREAD

   1   package (8 ounces) cream
         cheese, softened
   2   cups (8 ounces) shredded sharp
         Cheddar cheese
   5   tablespoons port wine
   1/4 cup finely chopped walnuts

   Process cream cheese, Cheddar cheese,
and wine in a food processor until
smooth. Spoon cheese mixture into an
airtight container; store in refrigerator.
   To give, sprinkle walnuts over cheese,
pressing walnuts lightly into cheese.
Yield: about 2 cups cheese spread

CHEESE BASKETS

For each basket, you will need red and
green acrylic paint, paintbrush, round
basket with handle and diagonally set
reeds, yellow grosgrain ribbon same
width as basket rim, 1"w yellow grosgrain
ribbon for bow, glue, 6" length of floral
wire, artificial greenery (we used silk
leaves with berries), fabric for basket
liner, small clay flowerpot, green
cellophane, and plastic wrap.
For tag, you will *also* need one 2" x 3"
piece each of poster board and fabric to
match basket liner, 1" x 2½" piece of
cream-colored paper, and a black
permanent fine-point marker.

*Follow Painting Techniques, page 122,
for painting tips. Allow paint to dry
after each application.*

1. Paint handle, inside of basket, and
every other reed on outside of basket red;
paint alternating reeds green.
2. Referring to Fig. 1, measure length of
handle and around one side of basket
rim; add 8". Using ribbon same width as
rim of basket, cut two lengths of ribbon
the determined measurement.

Fig. 1

3. Glue one end of one ribbon length at
center top of handle. Wrap ribbon around
handle three times to rim, glue around
one side of rim, wrap around opposite
side of handle three times, and glue
remaining end to center top of handle.
Repeat with remaining ribbon length in
opposite direction.
4. Using ribbon for bow and folding
ribbon away from you to form loops, fold
one end of ribbon to form desired-size
top loop; gather ribbon between fingers
(Fig. 2). Form another top loop and
gather ribbon between fingers (Fig. 3).
For bottom loops, form two loops slightly
larger than top loops; gather ribbon
between fingers.

Fig. 2   Fig. 3

 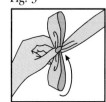

5. For streamers, multiply desired length
of streamers by 2; add 1". Form a loop
the determined measurement and gather
ribbon firmly between fingers; trim end.
Wrap wire around center of bow and twist
to secure. Cut loop in half (Fig. 4).

Fig. 4

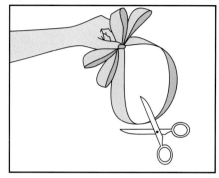

6. Arrange and glue bow and streamers
along handle.
7. For bow center, measure around
handle and center of bow; add 1".
Cut a length of ribbon the determined
measurement. Wrap ribbon around center
of bow and handle, overlapping ends
under handle; glue ends to secure. Glue
greenery to top of bow.
8. Follow *Making a Basket Liner,*
page 123, to make liner with an
unfinished edge.
9. Paint flowerpot green.
10. Measure around flowerpot; add ½".
Cut a length of ribbon the determined
measurement. Overlapping ends, glue
ribbon around rim of flowerpot. Glue silk
leaves and berries to ribbon at overlap.
11. Line flowerpot with cellophane, then
plastic wrap. Spoon cheese spread in
flowerpot; cover with plastic wrap. Cut an
18" length of ribbon. Gather cellophane
over cheese spread and tie ribbon into a
bow around gathers.
12. For tag, glue fabric piece to poster
board. Center and glue cream-colored
paper piece to fabric. Use marker to write
"Port Wine Cheese Spread" on tag.

SPICY HOLIDAY PECANS

*P*repared in minutes, *Peppery Pecans are sure to be a favorite. The savory nuts, spiced with red pepper, make zesty gifts for your best chums! Just scoop them into Christmas tree tins tied with ribbon.*

PEPPERY PECANS

  4   cups pecan halves
$1/3$ cup butter or margarine, melted
  1   tablespoon Worcestershire sauce
  1   teaspoon salt
$3/4$ teaspoon ground red pepper
$3/4$ teaspoon ground black pepper

Preheat oven to 300 degrees. Place pecans on an ungreased jellyroll pan. In a small bowl, combine melted butter, Worcestershire sauce, salt, red pepper, and black pepper. Pour mixture over pecans; stir to coat. Spread pecans in a single layer. Bake 15 minutes, stirring every 5 minutes. Cool on pan. Store in an airtight container.

Yield: about 4 cups pecans

For Celia
From Patti

PARTY PUNCH

A tangy drink that's great served hot or cold, Cranberry Spice Punch captures a blend of fabulous holiday flavors. For an elegant gift, present a bottle of this Christmas refreshment in an easy-to-make velvet bag tied with gold cord and accented with a pretty ornament.

CRANBERRY SPICE PUNCH

1 container (64 ounces) cranberry juice cocktail
1 can (46 ounces) pineapple juice
1 can (12 ounces) frozen lemonade concentrate, thawed
$1/2$ cup firmly packed brown sugar
2 cinnamon sticks
$1/2$ teaspoon whole cloves
$1/2$ teaspoon whole allspice
$1/8$ teaspoon salt

In a Dutch oven, combine cranberry juice cocktail, pineapple juice, lemonade concentrate, brown sugar, cinnamon sticks, cloves, allspice, and salt. Bring mixture to a boil over medium-high heat. Reduce heat to medium-low and simmer 5 minutes. Allow mixture to cool. Strain into a large container. Cover and store in refrigerator. Serve hot or cold.

Yield: about 16³/4 cups punch

ELEGANT BOTTLE BAG

You will need a 7¹/4" x 32¹/2" piece of crushed velvet, 750ml decorative bottle, 38" length of decorative cord, and an ornament with hanging loop.

Matching right sides and short edges, fold velvet in half. Using a ¹/4" seam allowance, sew sides of bag together.
2. Press top edge of bag ¹/4" to wrong side. Press ¹/4" to wrong side again and stitch in place.

3. Turn bag right side out. Place bottle in bag. Thread cord through hanging loop of ornament. Knot each end of cord. Tie cord into a bow around bag.

POP-IN-THE-OVEN BISCUITS

*Y*ou do the mixing and
kneading — all your friends
have to do is the baking!
Our Freezer Biscuits are a
perfect gift for the holidays
because they're ready to pop
right in the oven on hectic
mornings. For a special
remembrance, cross stitch
our festive holiday design on
a bread cloth to accompany
the convenient gift.

FREEZER BISCUITS

*These biscuits are an easy make-ahead
gift.*

   4   cups all-purpose flour
   2   tablespoons baking powder
1¹/₂   teaspoons salt
   1   teaspoon sugar
 ¹/₂   teaspoon baking soda
   1   container (16 ounces) sour cream
 ¹/₂   cup chilled butter, cut into pieces
   3   teaspoons water

In a large bowl, combine flour, baking
powder, salt, sugar, and baking soda.
Using a pastry blender or 2 knives, cut
sour cream and butter into dry
ingredients until mixture begins to cling
together. Add water, 1 teaspoonful at a
time, to moisten dough; shape into a ball.
On a lightly floured surface, use a floured
rolling pin to roll out dough to 1-inch
thickness. Use a 2-inch biscuit cutter to
cut out biscuits. Transfer to an ungreased
baking sheet. Cover and freeze 1 hour.
Transfer frozen biscuits to a resealable
plastic freezer bag. Give with baking
instructions.

Yield: about 2 dozen biscuits

To bake: Place frozen biscuits on an
ungreased baking sheet. Bake in a
425-degree oven 15 to 17 minutes or
until tops are lightly browned. Serve warm.

"SEASON'S GREETINGS" BREADCOVER

You will need embroidery floss (see
color key, page 110) and a White Royal
Classic Breadcover (14 ct).

*Refer to Cross Stitch and Embroidery
Stitches, page 123, before beginning
project.*

Using three strands of floss for *Cross
Stitch* and one strand for *Backstitch*,
and *French Knots*, stitch design,
page 110, on one corner of
breadcover ³/₄" from outer edge
of fringe.

HOLIDAY BUTTONS

*B*utton, button, who's
*g*ot the button? We have lots of
*t*hem, and they taste delightful!
*C*rowned with candied cherries,
*C*hristmas Button Cookies are
a cute way to make the merry
*y*uletide days even brighter.
A crafty fashion pin will be a
*m*emento of your kindness
*w*hen the snacks are gone.

CHRISTMAS BUTTON COOKIES

    1   cup butter or margarine, softened
    1   package (3 ounces) cream cheese,
          softened
    1   cup sugar
    1   egg yolk
    1   teaspoon almond extract
  2¹/₂ cups all-purpose flour
    1   package (4 ounces) red candied
          cherries
    1   package (4 ounces) green
          candied cherries

In a large bowl, cream butter, cream
cheese, and sugar until fluffy. Add egg
yolk and almond extract; beat until
smooth. Add flour to creamed mixture;
stir until a soft dough forms. Wrap in
plastic wrap and chill 1 hour.

Preheat oven to 325 degrees. Shape
dough into 1-inch balls and place
2 inches apart on a greased baking sheet.
Use thumb to make a slight indentation in
top of each ball. Bake 12 to 15 minutes
or until bottoms of cookies are lightly
browned. Press a candied cherry into
indentation in each warm cookie. Transfer
cookies to a wire rack to cool. Store in an
airtight container.

Yield: about 5¹/₂ dozen cookies

BUTTON TREE PIN

You will need tracing paper, two 3¹/₂"
squares of white felt, glue, one 3¹/₂"
square each of green fabric and red felt,
ten ³/₈" dia. buttons, red and black
embroidery floss, pin back, cellophane
bag, hole punch, and ⁷/₈"w wired ribbon.

1. Trace tree pattern, page 110, onto
tracing paper; cut out. Use pattern to cut
tree from one white felt piece.
2. Glue remaining white felt piece to
wrong side of fabric piece. Center and
glue tree on right side of fabric piece.
Leaving a ¹/₈" green fabric border, cut
out tree.

3. Use red floss to sew buttons to tree.
Use black floss to work *Straight Stitches*,
page 123, for details on trunk. Cut a 6"
length of red floss; tie into a bow. Glue
bow to top of trunk.
4. Center and glue tree on red felt.
Leaving a ¹/₈" red felt border, cut out tree.
Glue pin back to back of tree.
5. Place cookies in bag. Fold bag 3¹/₄" to
back. Punch two holes 1" apart in folded
part of bag. Thread ribbon length through
holes and tie into a bow at front. Attach
tree pin to bag below knot of bow.

FABULOUS FUDGE

Distinctive flavors make our scrumptious Chocolate-Sour Cream Fudge and Peanut Butter-Banana Fudge absolutely fabulous! These rich treats make great offerings for neighbors and friends when presented in papier-mâché boxes decorated with holiday designs cut from craft foam.

CHOCOLATE-SOUR CREAM FUDGE

    3 cups sugar
    1 container (8 ounces) sour cream
  1/3 cup cocoa
  1/3 cup light corn syrup
  1/4 cup butter or margarine
  1/4 teaspoon salt
    2 teaspoons vanilla extract
    1 cup chopped pecans

Line a 7 x 11-inch baking pan with aluminum foil, extending foil over ends of pan; grease foil. Butter sides of a heavy large saucepan. Combine sugar, sour cream, cocoa, corn syrup, butter, and salt in pan. Stirring constantly, cook over medium-low heat until sugar dissolves. Using a pastry brush dipped in hot water, wash down any sugar crystals on sides of pan. Attach a candy thermometer to pan, making sure thermometer does not touch bottom of pan. Increase heat to medium and bring to a boil. Cook, without stirring, until mixture reaches soft-ball stage (approximately 234 to 240 degrees). Test about 1/2 teaspoon mixture in ice water. Mixture should easily form a ball in ice water but flatten when held in your hand. Place pan in 2 inches of cold water in sink. Add vanilla; do not stir. Cool to approximately 110 degrees. Remove from sink. Using medium speed of an electric mixer, beat about 4 minutes or until fudge thickens and begins to lose its gloss. Stir in pecans. Pour into prepared pan. Cool completely. Use ends of foil to lift fudge from pan. Cut into 1-inch squares. Store in an airtight container in refrigerator.

Yield: about 5 dozen pieces fudge

PEANUT BUTTER-BANANA FUDGE

    2 cups firmly packed brown sugar
    1 cup granulated sugar
    1 cup evaporated milk
  1/2 cup butter or margarine
    1 package (10 ounces) peanut
       butter chips
    1 jar (7 ounces) marshmallow creme
    1 cup chopped peanuts
  1/2 teaspoon banana flavoring
  1/2 teaspoon vanilla extract

Line a 7 x 11-inch baking pan with aluminum foil, extending foil over ends of pan; grease foil. In a heavy large saucepan, combine sugars, evaporated milk, and butter. Attach a candy thermometer to pan, making sure thermometer does not touch bottom of pan. Stirring constantly, cook over medium heat until mixture reaches soft-ball stage (approximately 234 to 240). Test 1/2 teaspoon mixture in ice water. Mixture will easily form a ball in ice water but will flatten when held in your hand. Remove from heat and stir in peanut butter chips, marshmallow creme, peanuts, banana flavoring, and vanilla; stir until well blended. Pour into prepared pan. Cool completely. Use ends of foil to lift fudge from pan. Cut into 1-inch squares. Store in an airtight container in refrigerator.

Yield: about 5 dozen pieces fudge

A TRIO OF BOXES

For each box, you will need white spray primer, white spray paint, green and red craft foam, hole punch, and glue.
For star box, you will *also* need a 3 3/4" star-shaped papier-mâché box with lid.
For tree box, you will *also* need a 3" x 5" papier-mâché box with lid, tracing paper, and black craft foam.
For snowman box, you will *also* need a 3 1/4" x 4 1/4" oval papier-mâché box with lid, tracing paper, black and orange craft foam, and one each black permanent medium-point and fine-point markers.

1. For each box, spray box lid with primer, then paint, allowing to dry between applications.
2. For star box, trace around lid on red craft foam. Cut out 1/4" inside drawn line. Center and glue star to lid. Punch dots from green craft foam; glue dots to star.
3. For tree box, trace tree patterns, page 108, onto tracing paper; cut out. Use patterns to cut one tree top, tree center, and tree bottom from green craft foam and one trunk from black craft foam. Overlapping as necessary, glue shapes to lid top. Punch dots from red craft foam; glue dots to tree.
4. For snowman box, trace snowman patterns, page 108, onto tracing paper; cut out. Use patterns to cut one hat from black craft foam, one nose from orange craft foam, and one leaf from green craft foam. Use hole punch to punch two eyes from black craft foam and three berries from red craft foam. Arrange shapes on lid top; glue in place. Use fine-point marker to draw detail lines on leaf and nose. Use medium-point marker to draw mouth on lid.

SWEET DELIVERY

*K*eep your gift-giving "short" and sweet with Chocolate-Coconut Shortbread Wedges. For delivery, just draw a peppermint candy design on one cardboard cake circle and use another one for the bottom of your package. Place the nutty baked goodies between the circles and wrap it all in clear cellophane for a quick and clever gift!

CHOCOLATE-COCONUT SHORTBREAD WEDGES

- 1^1/$_2$ cups flaked coconut
- 1^1/$_2$ cups slivered almonds, toasted
- 1 cup butter, softened
- ^{2}/$_3$ cup sugar
- 1^1/$_2$ teaspoons vanilla extract
- 1^2/$_3$ cups all-purpose flour
- ^{1}/$_3$ cup cocoa
- ^{1}/$_2$ teaspoon salt

Preheat oven to 350 degrees. Process coconut and almonds in a food processor until coarsely ground. In a medium bowl, cream butter and sugar until fluffy. Beat in vanilla. In a small bowl, combine flour, cocoa, and salt. Gradually add dry ingredients; beat just until blended. Stir in coconut mixture. Divide dough into thirds. Pat each third of dough into a 7-inch-diameter circle on a baking sheet lined with parchment paper. Bake 25 to 30 minutes or until firm. Transfer baking sheet to a wire rack; cool 10 minutes. Transfer shortbread on paper to a firm surface. Cut each warm shortbread into 8 wedges; cool completely. Store in an airtight container.

Yield: 2 dozen shortbread wedges

PEPPERMINT CANDY WRAP

You will need red permanent broad-tip marker, two 8" cardboard cake circles, 20" x 25" piece of clear cellophane, transparent tape, and two 23" lengths of ^{7}/$_8$"w red satin ribbon.

1. Use marker to draw peppermint candy design on white side of one cake circle.

2. With drawn design on top, place shortbread between cake circles.
3. Place layered circles design side down at center of cellophane. Fold long edges of cellophane over circles; tape to secure. Gather cellophane at opposite sides. Tie ribbon into a bow around gathers.

SLICE-AND-BAKE COOKIE KIT

*K*ids love baking and decorating their own Christmas cookies, especially when you pack everything they need to make them into one fun carrier! Complete with purchased icing, sprinkles, and a nifty kid-size apron, our cookie kit will provide hours of fun. Don't forget to tuck in the most important ingredient — a roll of made-ahead Slice-and-Bake Cookie dough!

SLICE-AND-BAKE COOKIES

   3/4 cup butter or margarine, softened
1 1/4 cups sugar
     1 egg
     1 teaspoon vanilla extract
     2 cups all-purpose flour
   1/2 teaspoon salt

In a large bowl, cream butter and sugar until fluffy. Add egg and vanilla; beat until smooth. In a small bowl, combine flour and salt. Add dry ingredients to creamed mixture; stir until a soft dough forms. Divide dough in half. Place each half on plastic wrap. Use plastic wrap to shape dough into two 8-inch-long rolls. Chill 3 hours or until firm (if rolls have flattened, reshape into a round shape). Give with baking instructions.

To bake: Preheat oven to 375 degrees. Cut dough into 1/4-inch slices. Place 1 inch apart on a lightly greased baking sheet. Bake 6 to 8 minutes or until bottoms are lightly browned. Transfer cookies to a wire rack to cool. Store in an airtight container.

Yield: about 2 1/2 dozen cookies in each roll

COOKIE KIT

You will need a six-pack beverage carrier, red spray paint, Christmas-motif wrapping paper, spray adhesive, assorted cookie baking supplies (we used four jars of sprinkles, three tubes of decorating icing, decorating tips, and an apron), two 5" x 10" cellophane bags, and curling ribbon.

For gift tag, you will *also* need decorative-edge craft scissors, white paper, glue, hole punch, and a red permanent medium-point marker.

1. Spray paint carrier red.
2. Measure around carrier; add 1/2". Measure height of carrier sides. Cut a piece of wrapping paper the determined measurements. Apply spray adhesive to wrong side of wrapping paper. Overlapping ends at one side edge, glue wrapping paper around carrier.
3. Place desired baking supplies in cellophane bags. Tie several lengths of ribbon into a bow around top of each bag; curl ends. Place bags and remaining supplies in separate sections of carrier.
4. For tag, use craft scissors to cut a 1 1/4" x 3 3/4" piece from white paper. Punch hole in corner of tag.
5. Cut one motif from wrapping paper; glue to tag. Use marker to write message on tag. Thread curling ribbon through hole in tag; tie tag to gift. Curl ribbon ends.

ELEGANT PUMPKIN PIE

A luscious variation of a traditional holiday dessert, our Creamy Pumpkin Pie tastes as light and fluffy as it looks! Present it in a pie carrier embellished with an elegant ornament that will serve as a classy keepsake.

CREAMY PUMPKIN PIE

    1   can (15 ounces) pumpkin
    2   tablespoons dark corn syrup
 1 1/2 teaspoons pumpkin pie spice
  1/4   teaspoon salt
    1   envelope unflavored gelatin
  1/4   cup cold water
    1   package (3.4 ounces) French
        vanilla instant pudding mix
    1   cup milk
    1   container (8 ounces) frozen
        non-dairy whipped topping,
        thawed
    1   baked 9-inch pie crust

In a large bowl, combine pumpkin, corn syrup, pumpkin pie spice, and salt; beat until smooth. In a small saucepan, sprinkle gelatin over water; let stand 1 minute. Stirring constantly, cook over low heat about 5 minutes or until gelatin dissolves. In a medium bowl, add pudding mix to milk; beat until thickened. Add pudding and gelatin to pumpkin mixture; beat until smooth. Fold in topping. Spoon filling into crust. Cover and chill 3 hours or until firm.

Yield: about 8 servings

DECORATED PIE CARRIER

You will need a silver paint pen, glass ornament with hanging loop, 1 yd. each

of 1 1/2"w copper sheer wired ribbon and silver cord, floral wire, wire cutters, 6" length of gold cord, 1/4"w gold sheer wired ribbon, and a pie carrier with handle.

1. Use paint pen to paint design on ornament (we painted holly leaves with berries and "NOEL" on our ornament).
2. Follow *Making a Bow*, page 121, to make one copper ribbon bow with four 6" loops and two 3" streamers and one silver cord bow with four 6" loops and two 5" streamers. Knot each end of silver cord.
3. For hanger, thread gold cord through hanging loop of ornament; knot ends together.
4. Aligning centers, place bows at top of handle; secure with wire. Thread gold ribbon through hanger and tie into a bow around handle and bow centers.

ORANGE CANDY CAKE

A childhood favorite, orange slice candies make a great addition to a cake that's already delicious. Packed with homestyle flavor, the cake gets its moist texture from a "secret" ingredient — applesauce! Bestow the dessert with a hand-stamped card to spread your Yuletide greetings.

ORANGE SLICE CAKE

This cake slices better after sitting overnight.

   1 package (18 ounces) orange slice candies, finely chopped
   3 cups all-purpose flour, divided
   1 teaspoon ground cinnamon
   1 teaspoon salt
$^1/_2$ teaspoon ground cloves
   1 cup butter or margarine, softened
   1 cup sugar
   2 eggs, beaten
   1 teaspoon baking soda dissolved in 1 teaspoon hot water
$1^1/_2$ cups sweetened applesauce
$1^1/_2$ cups chopped pecans

Preheat oven to 350 degrees. In a medium bowl, combine candies and 1 cup flour; stir until well coated. Set aside. In a small bowl, combine remaining 2 cups flour, cinnamon, salt, and cloves. In a large bowl, cream butter and sugar until fluffy. Add eggs and baking soda mixture; beat until smooth. Add dry ingredients to creamed mixture; stir until well blended. Alternately stir gumdrop mixture and applesauce into batter, stirring until well blended. Stir in pecans.

Spoon batter into a greased 10-inch fluted tube pan. Bake 1 to $1^1/_4$ hours or until a toothpick inserted in center of cake comes out clean. Cool cake in pan 10 minutes. Place on a wire rack to cool completely. Store in an airtight container.

Yield: about 16 servings

HANDMADE CARD

You will need a gold paint pen, ruler, 5" x 7" stationery card, Christmas-motif rubber stamp, gold stamp pad, 1 yd. of $1^1/_2$"w wired ribbon, floral wire, wire cutters, and glue.

1. Use paint pen and ruler to draw a line $^3/_8$" inside each edge on front of card.
2. Stamp design along bottom edge of card.
3. Using ribbon, follow *Making a Bow*, page 121, to make a bow with four $5^1/_2$" loops and two $4^1/_2$" streamers. Glue bow to card $^1/_2$" from line drawn along long folded edge.

A "SOUP-ER" GIFT

To serve: Rinse and sort dried beans. In a large Dutch oven, combine beans and 12 cups water. Cover and bring to a boil over medium-high heat. Reduce heat to medium-low and cook 1 to 1 ¼ hours. Stir in seasoning mix, pasta, 2 cans (14½ ounces each) diced tomatoes, and 1 can (8 ounces) tomato sauce. Cover and simmer 30 minutes or until beans are tender. Serve warm.

*H*ere's a "soup-er" gift idea for the holidays! Include dressed-up bags of dried beans and pasta in a pretty gift basket along with a jar of zesty Italian seasoning mix. By adding only a few basic ingredients, your friends can sit down to a hot and hearty meal any time.

PASTA FAGIOLI SOUP MIX

- 2 tablespoons dried minced onion
- 1 tablespoon dried parsley flakes
- 1 tablespoon sugar
- 1 tablespoon celery salt
- 1 tablespoon sweet pepper flakes
- 2 teaspoons chicken bouillon granules
- 2 teaspoons dried Italian seasoning
- 1 1/2 teaspoons salt
- 1/2 teaspoon paprika
- 1/2 teaspoon garlic powder
- 1/2 teaspoon ground black pepper
- 1 package (16 ounces) dried cranberry beans and 1 cup ditalini pasta to give

In a small bowl, combine minced onion, parsley flakes, sugar, celery salt, pepper flakes, chicken bouillon, Italian seasoning, salt, paprika, garlic powder, and black pepper. Pour seasoning mix into a small jar with lid. Place beans and pasta in separate plastic bags. Give seasoning mix, beans, and pasta with serving instructions.

Yield: about 1/2 cup seasoning mix

To serve: Rinse and sort dried beans. In a large Dutch oven, combine beans and 12 cups water. Cover and bring to a boil over medium-high heat. Reduce heat to medium-low and cook 1 1/4 hours. Stir in seasoning mix, pasta, 2 cans (14 1/2 ounces each) diced tomatoes, and 1 can (8 ounces) tomato sauce. Cover and simmer 30 minutes or until beans are tender. Serve warm.

Yield: about 13 cups soup

SOUP MIX BAGS

You will need an 8 1/4" x 25 1/2" piece each of red and green fabric, pinking shears, two 5" x 8" pieces each of paper-backed fusible web and cream fabric, tracing paper, transfer paper, green and black permanent markers, raffia, natural excelsior, and a basket.

For gift tag, you will *also* need photocopy of serving instructions (page 107), glue, cream-colored paper, and serrated-edge craft scissors.

1. For each bag, matching right sides and short edges, fold 8 1/4" x 25 1/2" fabric pieces in half. Using a 1/4" seam allowance, sew sides of bag together. Use pinking shears to trim top edge of bag.
2. Fuse web to wrong side of cream fabric. Use pinking shears to cut two 2" x 3 1/2" labels from fused fabric.
3. Trace BEANS and PASTA patterns, page 107, onto tracing paper. Use transfer paper to transfer one pattern to each label. Use green marker to color "trees" and black marker to draw over transferred words and to add dots on trees and "stitches" along inside of label.
4. Arrange one label on each bag; fuse in place.
5. Place plastic bags of beans and pasta in corresponding fabric bags. Tie several lengths of raffia into a bow around top of bag.
6. Place excelsior, seasoning mix, and bags in basket.
7. For gift tag, glue serving instructions to cream paper. Leaving a 1/4" cream border, use craft scissors to cut out tag.

SANTA'S TRAVELIN' TRAIL MIX

*S*anta Claus is on his way — with lots of trail mix on his sleigh! Our recipe is full of sweet, energy-packed ingredients that will help busy folks keep going on hectic days. A map of the jolly old elf's "stops" makes a fitting decoration for a brightly colored gift bag.

SANTA'S TRAIL MIX

1 package (16 ounces) red and green candy-coated chocolate-covered peanuts
1 package (15.4 ounces) chocolate-covered raisins
2 packages (7$\frac{1}{2}$ ounces each) white fudge-covered pretzels
6 cups cinnamon graham cereal

In a very large bowl, combine peanuts, raisins, pretzels, and cereal. Store in an airtight container in a cool place.

Yield: about 16 cups mix

TRAIL MIX BAG

You will need a gift bag with handles, road map, red permanent medium-point marker, glue, and $\frac{7}{8}$"w satin ribbon. *For tag,* you will *also* need white and red paper and decorative-edge craft scissors.

1. Measure front of bag. Cut a piece from road map 2" smaller than front of bag. Center and glue map piece to front of bag. Tie ribbon into a bow around handle.
2. Use marker to draw "Santa's Trail" on map with circled X's to designate Santa's stops.

3. For tag, cut a 1$\frac{3}{4}$" x 3" piece from white paper. Use marker to write "SANTA'S TRAIL MIX He's on his way!!!" on tag. Glue tag to red paper. Leaving a $\frac{1}{4}$" red border, use craft scissors to cut out tag; glue tag to bag.

PEANUTTY "TREE-TS"

*S*hare season's greetings with all your pals when you give our Peanut Butter Crumb Cookies! With their hearty flavor and crunchy texture, these delicious goodies will be loved by all. For a really spirited "tree-t," offer your homemade cookies in gift bags adorned with evergreens cut from assorted holiday fabrics.

PEANUT BUTTER CRUMB COOKIES

 1   cup butter or margarine, softened
 1   cup extra-crunchy peanut butter
 $3/4$ cup firmly packed brown sugar
 $3/4$ cup granulated sugar
 2   eggs
 $1^{1}/2$ teaspoons vanilla extract
 $2^{1}/2$ cups all-purpose flour
 1   teaspoon baking powder
 1   teaspoon baking soda
 $1/2$ teaspoon salt
 $1^{1}/2$ cups coarsely crushed cinnamon graham crackers (about 22 squares), divided
 $1/2$ cup finely chopped dry-roasted peanuts

Preheat oven to 350 degrees. In a large bowl, cream butter, peanut butter, and sugars until fluffy. Add eggs and vanilla; beat until smooth. In a medium bowl, combine flour, baking powder, baking soda, and salt. Add dry ingredients to creamed mixture; beat until well blended. Stir in 1 cup cracker crumbs. In a small bowl, combine remaining $1/2$ cup cracker crumbs and peanuts. Roll heaping teaspoonfuls of dough into balls; roll in crumb mixture. Place balls on a lightly

greased baking sheet; flatten with a fork. Bake 7 to 9 minutes or until lightly browned. Transfer to a wire rack to cool. Store in an airtight container.

Yield: about 7 dozen cookies

CHRISTMAS TREE GIFT BAGS

For each bag, you will need paper-backed fusible web, gold and assorted green fabrics for appliqués, poster board, glue, and a white lunch-size paper bag.

1. Use patterns, page 111, and follow *Making Appliqués*, page 122, to make one star appliqué from gold fabric and one each of tree sections A, B, C, and D from green fabrics. Fuse appliqués to poster board; cut out.

2. Apply a thin line of glue on wrong side of each section along straight edge. Beginning with section D and overlapping sections $1/4$", arrange and glue tree sections on front of bag. Glue star to top of tree.

3. Place gift in bag. Fold bag $2^{1}/4$" to back. Fold corners back to form point at top of bag; glue to secure.

SANTA'S BUTTER CRUNCH PRETZELS

Wonderful for a party, family time in front of the television, or any other snacking occasion, Butter Crunch Pretzels are both salty and sweet! Offer our delightful snacks packed in an inventive fabric bag sporting the face of jolly old Saint Nick. Any merry muncher is sure to love this crunchy and crafty gift!

BUTTER CRUNCH PRETZELS

16 cups small pretzel twists
 1 cup firmly packed brown sugar
¹/₂ cup butter or margarine
¹/₄ cup light corn syrup
 1 teaspoon vanilla-butter-nut flavoring
¹/₂ teaspoon baking soda

Preheat oven to 200 degrees. Place pretzels in a large roasting pan. Butter sides of a heavy medium saucepan. Combine brown sugar, butter, and corn syrup in saucepan. Stirring constantly, cook over medium-low heat until sugar dissolves. Increase heat to medium and bring to a boil. Cook, without stirring, 5 minutes. Remove from heat. Stir in vanilla-butter-nut flavoring and baking soda (syrup will foam). Pour syrup over pretzels; stir until pretzels are well coated. Bake 1 hour, stirring every 15 minutes. Spread on greased aluminum foil to cool. Store in an airtight container.

Yield: about 20 cups pretzels

SANTA BAG

You will need a 3¹/₂" x 10" flesh-colored fabric piece, 3³/₄" x 10" and 7" square red fabric pieces, 10" x 17" white fabric piece, tracing paper, white and red felt, two ⁵/₈" dia. buttons for eyes, 12" length of ³/₈"w green satin ribbon, ³/₄" dia. jingle bell, 1" square of hook and loop fastener, and glue.

For all sewing steps, match right sides and raw edges and use a ¹/₄" seam allowance.

1. Matching long edges, sew flesh-colored fabric piece and 3³/₄" x 10" red fabric piece together; sew remaining long edge of flesh-colored fabric piece to white fabric piece.
2. Matching short edges, fold pieced fabric in half; finger press folded edge (bottom of bag). Sew sides of bag together.
3. Match each side seam along fold line at bottom of bag; sew across each corner 1¹/₂" from point (Fig. 1).

Fig. 1

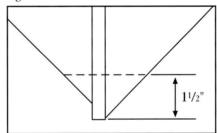

4. Turn bag right side out.
5. Trace patterns, page 110, onto tracing paper. Use patterns to cut nose and mouth shapes from red felt and two each of eyebrow and mustache shapes from white felt. Arrange and glue felt shapes and buttons on front of bag.
6. For hat, fold two adjacent sides of red fabric square ¹/₄" to wrong side; stitch in place. Matching right sides and stitched edges, fold square in half diagonally. Sew raw edges together. Turn right side out.
7. Press top edge of bag ¹/₄" to wrong side. Center open end of hat along back edge of bag (Fig. 2) and baste in place.

Fig. 2

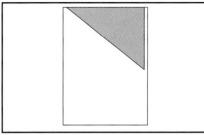

8. Press top edge of bag ¹/₄" to wrong side again and stitch in place. Tie ribbon into a bow. Sew ribbon and bell to tip of hat.
9. For bag closure, center and glue hook and loop fastener between inside top edges of bag.

HOLIDAY CHOCOLATES

*H*oliday chocolates are even more delicious when they're flavored with a hint of orange and molded in shapes befitting the Yuletide season. Present these creamy gifts in a papier-mâché box embellished with seasonal fabric, greenery, and a realistic "chocolate" Santa.

ORANGE CHOCOLATES

$1/2$ cup semisweet chocolate chips

9 ounces chocolate candy coating, chopped

$1/8$ teaspoon orange-flavored oil (used in candy making)

Vegetable cooking spray

Place chocolate chips, candy coating, and oil in top of a double boiler. Stirring frequently, cook over hot, not simmering, water until chocolate melts. Remove double boiler from heat, leaving chocolate over hot water. Lightly spray a $1^1/2$ x 3-inch metal candy mold with cooking spray. Spoon about 2 teaspoons chocolate into mold. Tap mold on counter to release air bubbles. Place mold on a baking sheet and chill about 10 minutes or until chocolate hardens. Turn mold over; firmly tap on counter to release chocolate. Lightly spray mold with cooking spray between each use. Store chocolates in an airtight container in refrigerator.

Yield: about $1^1/2$ dozen candies

CANDY MOLD BOX

You will need plaster of paris, candy mold, brown acrylic paint, paintbrush,

clear matte acrylic spray sealer, pinking shears, $3^1/2$" x $5^1/2$" fabric piece, glue, 4" x 6" papier-mâché box with lid, 3" x 5" felt piece, four artificial leaves, and four artificial berries.

Allow paint and sealer to dry after each application.

Thoroughly clean and dry mold before reusing for candy making.

1. Follow manufacturer's instructions to prepare plaster. Use candy mold and plaster to make plaster shape; allow to dry.

2. Paint shape brown. Apply two to three coats of sealer.

3. Use pinking shears to trim edges of fabric piece. Center and glue fabric piece on top of box lid. Center and glue felt piece on fabric piece. Glue plaster shape to center of felt piece. Glue one leaf and one berry at each corner of felt piece.

MEXICAN CORN BREAD STARS

*S*pice up Christmas meals
with a basket of Super Mexican
Corn Bread. Best served warm,
this zesty alternative to ordinary
bread is sure to be a welcome
surprise at the dinner table,
especially when presented in
our bread basket lined with
corn fabric and a simple hand
stitched bread cloth.

SUPER MEXICAN CORN BREAD

    1   cup all-purpose flour
    3/4 cup yellow cornmeal
    1 1/2 teaspoons baking powder
    1   teaspoon sugar
    1   teaspoon salt
    1/2 teaspoon baking soda
    1   cup buttermilk
    1   cup (4 ounces) shredded sharp
         Cheddar cheese
    1   can (8 1/2 ounces) cream-style corn
    2   eggs, beaten
    1/4 cup vegetable oil
    2   tablespoons seeded and chopped
         jalapeño peppers
    6   slices bacon, cooked and crumbled

Preheat oven to 375 degrees. In a
medium bowl, combine flour, cornmeal,
baking powder, sugar, salt, and baking
soda. Stir in buttermilk, cheese, corn,
eggs, oil, peppers, and bacon. Pour into
4 1/2-inch-wide greased star-shaped baking
pans or greased muffin cups. Bake 25 to
30 minutes or until a toothpick inserted
in center of corn bread comes out clean.
Serve warm or cool completely. Store in
an airtight container.

Yield: about 8 corn bread stars or
15 muffins

STAR-BURST BREADCOVER

You will need paper-backed fusible
web; fabric scraps for appliqués;
18" square Charles Craft breadcover;
four 1/4" dia. buttons; red, green, and gold
embroidery floss; tracing paper; transfer
paper; torn piece of fabric slightly larger
than breadcover for basket liner; and a
basket (we used a 9" x 11" oval basket).

1. Use pattern, page 112, and follow
Making Appliqués, page 122, to make
four star appliqués from fabric scraps.
Fuse one star to each corner of
breadcover.

2. Use gold floss to sew one button at
center of each star and work *Running
Stitches,* page 123, along edges of
each star.

3. Trace embroidery pattern, page 112,
onto tracing paper. Use transfer paper to
lightly transfer pattern to corners of
breadcover around each star.

4. Use green floss to work *Straight
Stitches,* page 123, for leaves and red
floss to work *French Knots,* page 123,
for berries.

5. Center breadcover on basket liner and
place in basket.

Bright Cookie Ornaments

These Christmas "ornaments" are sure to brighten the holidays of those who receive them! The delightful honey-sweetened cookies are "painted" with colorful icings and cleverly packaged in a sectioned "ornament" box. What a fun and creative gift idea!

HONEY ORNAMENT COOKIES

COOKIES

- 1/2 cup butter or margarine, softened
- 1/3 cup vegetable shortening
- 1 cup sugar
- 1/4 cup honey
- 1 egg
- 1/2 teaspoon vanilla extract
- 3 cups all-purpose flour
- 1/4 teaspoon salt

ICING

- 6 2/3 cups sifted confectioners sugar
- 6 to 7 tablespoons water
- 1 tablespoon light corn syrup
- 1 teaspoon vanilla extract
  Red, green, yellow, and blue paste food coloring

Preheat oven to 350 degrees. Trace ornament patterns, page 111, onto stencil plastic; cut out. For cookies, cream butter, shortening, and sugar in a large bowl until fluffy. Add honey, egg, and vanilla; beat until smooth. In a medium bowl, combine flour and salt. Add dry ingredients to creamed mixture; stir until a soft dough forms. Divide dough in half. On a lightly floured surface, use a floured rolling pin to roll out half of dough to 1/8-inch thickness. Use patterns and a sharp knife to cut out cookies. Transfer to a greased baking sheet. Use a plastic drinking straw to cut a hole in top of each cookie. Bake 5 to 7 minutes or until bottoms are lightly browned. Transfer cookies to a wire rack to cool.

For icing, combine confectioners sugar, water, corn syrup, and vanilla in a medium bowl; stir until smooth. Divide icing into 5 small bowls. Tint red, green, yellow, and blue; leave remaining icing white. Spoon icing into pastry bags fitted with small round tips. Pipe outline of each color of designs onto cookies; fill in with icing. Let icing harden. Store in a single layer in an airtight container.

SECTIONED ORNAMENT BOX

You will need a gift box (we used an 8 1/4" x 11" x 1 1/2"h box), craft knife and cutting mat, cellophane, glue, poster board, white cupcake liners, white excelsior, and 1 1/4"w wired ribbon.

1. Remove lid from box. Place lid, top side down, on cutting mat. Draw a line on wrong side of lid 7/8" inside each side. Use craft knife to cut out opening.
2. Cut a piece of cellophane 1" larger than opening. Center and glue cellophane over opening on wrong side of lid.
3. For dividers, measure width and length of box. Measure depth of box; subtract 1/4". Cut two short dividers from poster board the determined width and depth measurement. Cut one long divider from poster board the determined length and depth measurement.
4. Mark center of each short divider. Mark long divider in three equal sections. Leaving 1/2" uncut, cut across each divider where marked.
5. Place long divider cut side up in center of box. Place short dividers cut side down over cuts in long divider.
6. Line sections of box with excelsior. Place one cupcake liner in each section of box; place cookies in liners. Replace lid. Wrapping ribbon around two opposite corners of box, tie ribbon into a bow around box.

CHRISTMAS RELISH

*T*he name of this recipe says it all! Easy Processor Relish is a breeze to make because the food processor does all the work. Carry gift jars of the quick and tasty condiment in cute spray painted cans accented with festive labels.

EASY PROCESSOR RELISH

  2 jars (32 ounces each) hamburger dill pickle slices, drained
  1 package (10 ounces) frozen chopped green peppers, thawed and drained
  1 cup frozen chopped onions, thawed and drained
  1 cup sugar
  1 jar (4 ounces) diced pimientos, drained
  1 tablespoon apple cider vinegar
  $1/2$ teaspoon salt
  $1/2$ teaspoon celery seed

Process pickles in a food processor until finely chopped. Drain chopped pickles. In a large bowl, combine pickles, green peppers, onions, sugar, pimientos, vinegar, salt, and celery seed; stir until well blended. Store in an airtight container in refrigerator.

Yield: about $5^3/4$ cups relish

GIFT CANS

For each can, you will need a $4^3/4$"h x $3^1/4$" dia. can, white spray primer, green spray paint, matte clear acrylic spray sealer, hammer, nail, 18" of 19-gauge wire, six red buttons, four

each of green and white buttons, pliers, wrapping paper, and glue.

For gift tag, you will *also* need colored pencils, photocopy of tag design (page 113), black permanent fine-point marker, red paper, and decorative-edge craft scissors.

1. Allowing to dry after each application, spray can with primer, paint, then sealer.
2. For handle, use hammer and nail to make a hole near rim on each side of can. Form a $1^1/4$" loop at center of wire length. Beginning and ending with a red button and alternating colors, thread seven buttons onto one wire end. Insert wire end into one hole in can. Use pliers to bend wire end up and around wire handle; twist end to secure. Repeat for opposite side.
3. Cut a $2^3/4$" x $11^1/2$" piece of wrapping paper. Overlapping ends at back, center and glue paper around can.
4. For gift tag, use pencils to color tag design; cut out. Use marker to write message on tag. Glue tag to red paper. Leaving a $1/4$" red border, use craft scissors to cut out gift tag. Glue tag to can.

SIMPLE STAR COOKIES

*S*imple, melt-in-your-
mouth Star Cookies are a
stellar holiday idea! Baked
to crispy perfection, these
classic delicacies are gathered
in easy-to-make felt drawstring
bags. Handmade tree ornaments
add pizzazz to your gift.

STAR COOKIES

3/4 cup butter or margarine, softened
1/2 cup sugar
1 egg
1 teaspoon vanilla extract
1 3/4 cups all-purpose flour
3 tablespoons cornstarch
1/2 teaspoon baking powder
1/8 teaspoon salt

Preheat oven to 350 degrees. In a
medium bowl, cream butter and sugar
until fluffy. Add egg and vanilla; beat until
smooth. In a small bowl, combine flour,
cornstarch, baking powder, and salt. Add
dry ingredients to creamed mixture; stir
until a soft dough forms. On a lightly
floured surface, use a floured rolling pin
to roll out dough to 1/8-inch thickness.
Use a 2 3/4-inch-wide scalloped-edge star-
shaped cookie cutter to cut out cookies.
Transfer to a greased baking sheet. Bake
8 to 9 minutes or until bottoms are lightly
browned. Transfer cookies to a wire rack
to cool. Store in an airtight container.
Yield: about 4 dozen cookies

FELT GIFT BAGS

For each bag, you will need two 9" x 12"
felt pieces; embroidery floss; pinking
shears; tracing paper; white, red, and
green felt scraps; glue; 7mm jingle bell;
and 18" of satin cord.

For each gift tag, you will *also* need
colored pencils, photocopy of tag design
(page 113), red permanent fine-point
marker, green paper, and a hole punch.

1. Matching edges, place 9" x 12" felt
pieces together.
2. Using floss and *Running Stitch*,
page 123, sew felt pieces together along
one short and two long edges. Use
pinking shears to trim edges of bag.
3. Trace small, medium, and large star
patterns, page 112, onto tracing paper;
cut out. Use small star pattern to cut one
star from felt scrap. Use patterns and
pinking shears to cut one large star and
one medium star from felt scraps.

4. Stacking stars from largest to smallest,
glue stars together. Glue bell to center of
small star.
5. For hanger, cut a 1/4" x 2" felt piece.
Glue short ends together. Glue ends of
hanger to back of large star.
6. For gift tag, use pencils to color tag
design; cut out. Use marker to write
message on tag. Glue tag to green paper.
Leaving a 1/8" green border, cut out tag.
Punch hole in corner of tag.
7. Place cookies in bag. Thread cord
through hanger and hole in gift tag. Tie
cord into a bow around top of bag;
knot ends.

CHEESY VEGGIE SPREAD

A *garden of flavors is yours to share when you whip up a batch of Fresh Vegetable Spread! This mix of crunchy chopped veggies and sharp Cheddar cheese is blended with mayonnaise and seasoned with Worcestershire sauce and lemon pepper. Pass it out with party bread in a festive fabric bag to share this refreshing snack with friends.*

FRESH VEGETABLE SPREAD

- 2 cups (8 ounces) finely shredded sharp Cheddar cheese
- 2 cups mayonnaise
- 1 tablespoon Worcestershire sauce
- 2 cloves garlic, minced
- 1/2 teaspoon lemon pepper
- 1 cup finely chopped green pepper
- 1 cup finely chopped onion
- 1 cup shredded carrots
- 1 cup shredded radishes
- 1 cup finely chopped celery
- 1 tablespoon finely chopped fresh parsley
- 1 loaf (12 ounces) cocktail bread to give

In a large bowl, combine Cheddar cheese and mayonnaise. Add Worcestershire sauce, garlic, and lemon pepper; stir until well blended. Stir in green pepper, onion, carrots, radishes, celery, and parsley. Spoon spread into pint jars. Cover and chill 2 hours to let flavors blend. Give with cocktail bread.

Yield: about 6 cups spread

FABRIC BAG

You will need a 9" x 36" piece of fabric, pinking shears, 1 yd. of 2"w wired ribbon, and artificial greenery (we used a holly stem with berries).

For gift tag, you will *also* need self-adhesive gift sticker, green paper, decorative-edge craft scissors, and a black permanent fine-point marker.

1. Matching right sides and short edges, fold fabric in half. Using a 1/2" seam allowance, sew sides of bag together. Use pinking shears to trim top edge of bag.
2. Place bread and spread in bag. Tie ribbon into a bow around top of bag. Tuck greenery under bow.
3. For gift tag, apply sticker to green paper. Leaving a 1/4" green border, use craft scissors to cut out gift tag. Use marker to write message on tag.

DELUXE CHOCOLATE CAKE

*N*o doubt about it, this rich Cherry-Chocolate Cake is like no other! Chunks of maraschino cherries make the moist cake a heavenly confection. Present it atop a clear plate that's hand-painted with elegant snowflake designs for a merry memento.

CHERRY-CHOCOLATE CAKE

1 package (18$^{1}/_{2}$ ounces) butter
     recipe yellow cake mix without
     pudding in the mix
$^{1}/_{3}$ cup sugar
3 tablespoons cocoa
1 cup buttermilk
3 eggs
$^{1}/_{2}$ cup vegetable oil
1 jar (16 ounces) maraschino
     cherries, drained and chopped

Do not preheat oven. In a large bowl, combine cake mix, sugar, and cocoa. Add buttermilk, eggs, and oil; beat at low speed of an electric mixer until blended. Beat at medium speed 5 minutes. Stir in cherries. Pour batter into a greased 10-inch fluted tube pan. Place pan in cold oven and set temperature at 325 degrees. Bake 1 to 1 hour 10 minutes or until a toothpick inserted in center of cake comes out clean. Cool cake in pan 10 minutes. Invert onto a wire rack to cool completely. Store in an airtight container.

Yield: about 16 servings

SNOWFLAKE CAKE PLATE

You will need tracing paper, removable tape, octagonal clear glass plate (we

used a 12" dia. plate), white Delta CeramDecor™ Air-Dry Perm Enamel™ paint, and a paintbrush.

Refer to Painting Techniques, page 122, for painting tips.

1. Trace snowflake and swirl patterns, page 112, separately onto tracing paper.
2. Tape patterns right side down on top of plate.

3. Working on wrong side of plate, paint snowflakes and swirls on plate.
4. Repeat Steps 2 and 3, moving patterns for desired placement of designs. Paint detail lines around edge of plate.
5. Remove patterns.
6. Hand wash plate after each use.

SPICY REINDEER TREAT

*W*hat a handsome fellow! This friendly cinnamon stick reindeer will be happy to escort a gift of hand-blended spices and a purchased cake mix. Combine the mixes and bake them, and you've got a quick and sumptuous holiday treat!

SPEEDY SPICE-NUT CAKE

1 teaspoon ground cinnamon
1/2 teaspoon ground nutmeg
1/2 teaspoon ground allspice
1/4 teaspoon ground cloves
1 cup chopped pecans
1 package (18 1/4 ounces) yellow cake mix to give

In a small bowl, combine cinnamon, nutmeg, allspice, and cloves. Stir in pecans. Transfer to a cellophane bag. Give with cake mix and baking instructions.

Yield: about 1 cup plus 2 tablespoons spice-nut mix

To bake: Grease a 10-inch fluted tube pan. Prepare and bake cake mix according to package directions, stirring in spice-nut mix. Cool in pan 10 minutes. Invert cake onto serving plate; serve warm or cool completely. Store in an airtight container.

Yield: about 16 servings

CINNAMON STICK REINDEER

You will need tracing paper, brown felt, scrap of black felt, pinking shears, glue, brown and black embroidery floss, two 3/8" dia. buttons, polyester fiberfill, long grain rice, heavy duty nylon thread, large-eye needle, six 1 3/4" and two 2 1/2" lengths of cinnamon stick, eight 3/8" dia. wooden beads, glue, twigs for antlers, 1" x 16" torn fabric strip, boxed cake mix, wrapping paper, and double-sided tape.

Match wrong sides and raw edges and stitch along edges of shapes to sew felt shapes together.

1. Trace reindeer patterns, page 114, onto tracing paper; cut out.
2. Use nose pattern to cut nose from black felt. Use remaining patterns and pinking shears to cut two each of head and body shapes and four ear shapes from brown felt.
3. Use six strands of black floss and work *Running Stitches*, page 123, for mouth and to stitch along edge of nose to sew nose to one head shape. Sew buttons to head shape for eyes.
4. For each ear, use three strands of brown floss and *Running Stitch* to sew two ear shapes together.
5. Place head shapes together. Pleating each ear at center, pin ear shapes between head shapes. Leaving an opening for stuffing, use three strands of brown floss and *Running Stitch* to sew head shapes together; remove pins. Stuff lightly with fiberfill; stitch opening closed.
6. Leaving bottom open for filling, use three strands of brown floss and *Running Stitch* to sew body shapes together. Fill body with rice; stitch opening closed.
7. For each back leg, leave a 2" tail of nylon thread and insert needle from back to front of body. Using one 1 3/4" and one 2 1/2" cinnamon stick, refer to Fig. 1 and

thread cinnamon sticks and beads onto thread; bring thread back through beads and cinnamon sticks and insert needle from front to back of body. Knot thread ends together. Repeat for each front leg, using two 1 3/4" cinnamon sticks.

Fig. 1

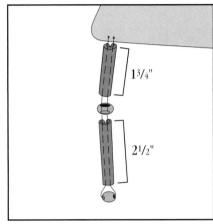

1 3/4"

2 1/2"

8. Sew head to body. Glue twigs to head.
9. Tie fabric strip around neck for scarf.
10. Using wrapping paper, wrap cake mix box like a package. Use tape to secure reindeer to package.

SNAPPY HORSERADISH DRESSING

A snappy complement for holiday fare — and even after the holidays — Creamy Horseradish Dressing is ideal for dipping or pouring over salads! Fill jars with this flavorful condiment and cover the lids with seasonal fabric circles. Place them in purchased gift bags tied with curling ribbon to spread your Yuletide cheer!

CREAMY HORSERADISH DRESSING

1   cup sour cream
$1/2$ cup buttermilk
$1/2$ cup mayonnaise
1   tablespoon prepared horseradish
1   tablespoon finely chopped green onion
1   teaspoon freshly squeezed lemon juice
$1/2$ teaspoon dry mustard
$1/4$ teaspoon salt

In a medium bowl, combine sour cream, buttermilk, mayonnaise, horseradish, green onion, lemon juice, dry mustard, and salt; stir until well blended. Store in an airtight container in refrigerator. Serve with salad greens or as a dip with vegetables.

Yield: about 2 cups dressing

GIFT BAG AND JAR LID COVER

You will need a gift bag, curling ribbon, jar with lid, fabric to cover jar lid, pinking shears, and a rubber band.

1. Draw around jar lid on wrong side of fabric. Use pinking shears to cut out circle 2" outside drawn line. Place fabric

circle over jar lid; secure with rubber band. Tie several lengths of curling ribbon around rubber band; curl ends.

2. Place gift in bag. Tie handles of bag together with several lengths of curling ribbon; curl ends.

TEACHER TREATS

*C*hildren will learn a lesson in thoughtfulness when they give crafty gift boxes filled with our Creamy Fruit and Nut Candies! Because the recipe makes plenty, they can shower all the teachers they know with Christmas offerings. Add personalized "chalkboard" labels to the apple-shaped boxes for an A⁺ touch.

CREAMY FRUIT AND NUT CANDIES

   1 cup chopped walnuts
   1 cup chopped pecans
   1 container (4 ounces) red candied cherries, chopped
   1 container (4 ounces) green candied cherries, chopped
   3 cups sugar
1¹/₂ cups half and half
 ¹/₄ cup light corn syrup
1¹/₂ teaspoons vanilla extract

In a large bowl, combine walnuts, pecans, and cherries; set aside. Line a 7 x 11-inch baking pan with aluminum foil, extending foil over ends of pan; grease foil. Butter sides of a heavy large saucepan. Combine sugar, half and half, and corn syrup in pan. Stirring constantly, cook over medium-low heat until sugar dissolves. Using a pastry brush dipped in hot water, wash down any sugar crystals on sides of pan. Attach a candy thermometer to pan, making sure thermometer does not touch bottom of pan. Increase heat to medium and bring to a boil. Cook, without stirring, until mixture reaches soft-ball stage (approximately 234 to 240 degrees). Test

about ¹/₂ teaspoon mixture in ice water. Mixture will easily form a ball in ice water but will flatten when held in your hand. Place pan in 2 inches of cold water in sink. Add vanilla; do not stir. Cool to approximately 110 degrees. Using medium speed of an electric mixture, beat about 4 minutes or until candy thickens and looks creamy. Stir in nut mixture. Press candy into prepared pan; let cool. Cover loosely with waxed paper. Let candy stand overnight at room temperature.

Use ends of foil to lift candy from pan. Cut into 1-inch squares. Store in an airtight container in a cool place.

Yield: about 5 dozen pieces candy

TEACHERS' GIFT BOXES WITH BLACKBOARD GIFT TAGS

For each box, you will need an apple-shaped papier-mâché box, artificial greenery (we used a sprig of holly leaves with berries), and glue.
For gift tag, you will *also* need black paper and a white colored pencil.

1. Glue greenery to stem of box lid.
2. For gift tag, cut a 2" square of black paper. Use pencil to write message on tag. Glue tag to box lid.

MINI SNOWBALL SNACKS

*D*usted *with a sweet layer of "snow," our Mini Snowball Snacks pack a chocolate-peanut butter crunch! These tasty tidbits are sure to be a hit when you deliver them in a white plastic bowl painted with the charming face of a snowman. Crown the frosty gentleman with a ribbon-trimmed top hat accented with a sprig of holly.*

MINI SNOWBALL SNACKS

     8 cups cocoa-flavored puff cereal
     1 package (10 ounces) peanut
          butter chips
    $1/2$ cup butter or margarine
     2 tablespoons light corn syrup
     3 cups sifted confectioners sugar

Place cereal in a large bowl. Combine peanut butter chips, butter, and corn syrup in a medium saucepan. Stirring constantly, cook over low heat until chips melt. Pour peanut butter mixture over cereal; stir until evenly coated. Pour about $1^1/2$ cups confectioners sugar into each of two 1-gallon resealable plastic bags. Add half of coated cereal to each bag. Gently shake each bag until mixture is evenly coated with sugar. Spread onto waxed paper; allow to cool completely. Store in a resealable plastic bag.

Yield: about 10 cups snacks

SNOWMAN BOWL

You will need tracing paper, transfer paper, $8^3/4$" dia. white plastic bowl with lid, black and orange paint pens, black permanent fine-point marker, 24" length of $1^1/2$"w ribbon, $8^3/4$" dia. party hat (including brim), glue, artificial greenery (we used a sprig of holly leaves with berries), and double-sided tape.

1. Trace face pattern, page 120, onto tracing paper. Use transfer paper to transfer face to outside of bowl.
2. Use paint pens to paint eyes and mouth black and nose orange. Use marker to outline and add detail lines to nose.
3. Remove lid; place snacks in bowl. Replace lid.
4. For hat band, glue ribbon around hat, overlapping ends. Glue greenery to ribbon. Use tape to temporarily secure hat on lid.

IN THE "MO-O-OD"

*T*o get your pals in the Christmas "mo-o-od," share our homemade Spicy Buttermilk Dressing. This smooth, creamy sauce is great on salads, and it also makes a terrific dip for chips! Make a fitting presentation by placing a hand-painted jar in a basket and adding a shiny cowbell.

SPICY BUTTERMILK DRESSING

- 1 cup mayonnaise
- 1 cup buttermilk
- 1 tablespoon chopped fresh parsley
- 1 tablespoon finely chopped onion
- 1 clove garlic, minced
- 1 teaspoon ground black pepper
- $^1/_2$ teaspoon ground cumin
- $^1/_4$ teaspoon ground red pepper

In a small bowl, whisk mayonnaise, buttermilk, parsley, onion, garlic, black pepper, cumin, and red pepper until smooth. Store in an airtight container in refrigerator.

Yield: about 2 cups dressing

COW JAR

You will need natural sponge pieces, black Delta CeramDecor™ Air-Dry Perm Enamel™ paint, paper towel, jar with lid, 31mm cowbell, $^3/_8$"w satin ribbon, green excelsior, glue, miniature ornament garland, and a basket large enough to accommodate jar.

For gift tag, you will *also* need decorative-edge craft scissors, green paper, and a black permanent medium-point marker.

1. Follow *Sponge Painting*, page 122, to paint spots on jar.
2. Measure around jar lid; add 14". Cut a length of ribbon the determined measurement. Thread bell onto ribbon. Tie ribbon into a bow around jar lid.
3. Place excelsior, then jar in basket.
4. Arrange garland around jar and basket; spot glue to secure.
5. Using craft scissors, cut a 1$^3/_4$" x 3" piece of green paper. Use marker to write message on tag and to draw "stitches" around message. Glue tag to basket.

Bake uncovered in a 350° oven 45 to 50 minutes or until heated through and top is golden brown. Enjoy!

A real time-saver, our Turkey and Dressing Casserole is a great heat-and-eat meal during the holidays! For a welcome gift, use clear cellophane and an ornament-accented bow to tie up the present with style.

TURKEY AND DRESSING CASSEROLE

- 4 cups chopped cooked turkey
- 8 ounces breakfast sausage, browned and crumbled
- 1/2 cup finely chopped onion
- 1/2 cup finely chopped celery
- 1/2 cup finely chopped green pepper
- 1/2 teaspoon ground black pepper
- 1 can (10 3/4 ounces) cream of chicken soup
- 1 container (8 ounces) sour cream
- 1/2 cup milk
- 1 package (8 ounces) corn bread stuffing
- 1/4 cup butter or margarine, melted
- 1/4 cup chicken broth
- 1/2 teaspoon rubbed sage
- 1 1/2 cups shredded white Cheddar cheese

In a large bowl, combine turkey, sausage, half of onion, half of celery, half of green pepper, and half of black pepper. In a small bowl, combine soup, sour cream, and milk; stir until well blended. Stir soup mixture into turkey mixture. Spoon into a greased 9 x 13-inch baking dish. In a medium bowl, combine stuffing, melted butter, chicken broth, sage, and remaining onion, celery, green pepper, and black pepper. Stir in Cheddar cheese. Spoon over turkey mixture. Cover and store in refrigerator. Give with baking instructions.

Yield: 6 to 8 servings

To bake: Bake uncovered in a 350-degree oven 45 to 50 minutes or until heated through and top is golden brown. Serve warm.

CASSEROLE WRAP WITH BOW AND ORNAMENT

For a 9" x 13" casserole dish, you will need 1 3/4"w wired ribbon, floral wire, wire cutters, 1 1/2 yds. of 30"w cellophane, 32" length of gold cord, double-sided tape, glue, artificial greenery (we used three sprigs of holly with berries), and a 5"h nutcracker ornament.

For tag, you will *also* need white paper, black permanent medium-point marker, green paper, decorative-edge craft scissors, hole punch, and a 6" length of gold cord.

1. Use wired ribbon and follow *Making a Bow*, page 121, to make bow with four 8" loops and two 4" streamers.
2. Place casserole dish at center of cellophane. Gather cellophane over top of casserole dish; tie gold cord around gathers. Tie a knot in each end of cord. Use tape to secure short edges of cellophane if necessary.
3. Tie ends of cord into a bow around center of ribbon bow. Glue greenery, then ornament to center of bow.
4. For tag, cut a 1 3/4" x 3 7/8" piece of white paper. Use marker to write baking instructions on tag. Glue tag to green paper. Leaving a 1/4" green border, use craft scissors to cut out tag. Punch hole in corner of tag. Thread 6" length of cord through hole and tie to bow.

"FIRE-Y" CINNAMON LOLLIPOPS

*E*veryone loves a lollipop, and the zippy flavor of cinnamon fits right in with the holidays! Our Cinnamon Christmas Lollipops are a yummy surprise, especially for kids with a sweet tooth. A sponge-painted paper bag "chimney," complete with a sign beckoning Santa, is ideal for packaging these sweet but "fire-y" candies-on-a-stick.

CINNAMON CHRISTMAS LOLLIPOPS

    Vegetable cooking spray
    Lollipop sticks
2 cups sugar
1 cup water
²/₃ cup light corn syrup
¹/₄ teaspoon cinnamon oil (used in candy making)
¹/₄ teaspoon red liquid food coloring
    Plastic lollipop bags and ribbon

Heavily spray a baking sheet with cooking spray. Place lollipop sticks about 3 inches apart on baking sheet. In a large saucepan, combine sugar, water, and corn syrup. Stirring constantly, cook over medium-low heat until sugar dissolves. Using a pastry brush dipped in hot water, wash down any sugar crystals on sides of pan. Attach a candy thermometer to pan, making sure thermometer does not touch bottom of pan. Increase heat to medium and bring to a boil. Cook, without stirring, until mixture reaches hard-crack stage (approximately 300 to 310 degrees). Test about ¹/₂ teaspoon mixture in ice water. Mixture will form brittle threads in ice water and will remain brittle when removed from the water. Remove from heat; stir in cinnamon oil and food coloring. Spoon 1 tablespoon hot candy syrup over 1 end of each lollipop stick to form a 2¹/₂-inch-diameter circle. Let candy cool. Place in individual plastic bags; tie with ribbon.

Yield: about 30 lollipops

CHIMNEY GIFT BAG

You will need compressed craft sponge, lunch-size white paper bag, and red acrylic paint.

For gift tag, you will *also* need tracing paper, transfer paper, poster board, black and red permanent fine-point markers, glue, red paper, 13" long stick, and a 14" length of ⁵/₈"w grosgrain ribbon.

1. Cut a 1" x 1³/₄" piece from sponge.
2. Leaving top 2¹/₂" of bag unpainted, follow *Sponge Painting,* page 122, to paint red bricks on bag.
3. Fold top of bag down 1¹/₂" to right side. Cut a sawtooth design along edge of bag to ¹/₂" from fold.
4. For gift tag, trace pattern, page 117, onto tracing paper. Use transfer paper to transfer design onto poster board. Cutting ¹/₈" outside transferred lines, cut out tag. Use black marker to draw over transferred words and red marker to draw over transferred lines on tag.
5. Glue tag to red paper. Leaving a ¹/₄" red border, cut out tag. Glue tag to stick. Tie ribbon into a bow; glue to bottom of tag.

GO BANANAS!

*Y*our friends will go bananas over our Banana Split Topping! Just a little of this delicious concoction will add the flavor of a banana split to all kinds of desserts — from ice cream to pound cake. An adorable snowman, created from a sock-covered jar of sauce and a foam ball, makes a cute presentation.

BANANA SPLIT TOPPING

- 1 can (21 ounces) cherry pie filling
- 1 jar (10 ounces) maraschino cherries
- 2 cans (15^1/$_4$ ounces each) pineapple tidbits in juice
- ^{1}/$_4$ cup firmly packed brown sugar
- 1 teaspoon almond extract
- 1 teaspoon banana flavoring

In a medium saucepan, combine pie filling, maraschino cherries, pineapple, and brown sugar. Stirring frequently, cook over medium heat about 10 minutes or until heated through. Remove from heat. Stir in almond extract and banana flavoring; cool. Store in an airtight container in refrigerator.

Yield: about 5^1/$_2$ cups topping

SNOWMAN JAR

You will need a 16-ounce jar with lid; child-size white sock; 3" dia. foam ball; glue; tracing paper; white, yellow, orange, red, green, and blue felt; pinking shears; white embroidery floss; ^{1}/$_2$" dia. button; two straight pins with 3mm black bead heads; three ^{3}/$_4$" dia. buttons; and a 1" square of hook and loop fastener.

1. Place jar in sock. Trim sock 1" above jar.
2. For head, cover ball with remaining portion of sock. Gather ends of sock around ball at top and bottom; glue to secure.
3. Trace nose and star patterns, page 114, onto tracing paper. Use patterns to cut one nose from orange felt and one star each from yellow and white felt. Use pinking shears to cut a 4^1/$_2$" x 10^1/$_2$" red felt piece for hat, ^{1}/$_2$" x 10^1/$_2$" green felt piece for hat brim, 1^1/$_2$" x 3^1/$_4$" blue felt piece for bow tie, and ^{3}/$_4$" x 1^1/$_2$" yellow felt piece for knot.
4. For hat, glue one long edge of red felt piece around center of head, overlapping ends at back. Gather hat over top of head. Tie a 6" length of floss into a knot around gathers. Use floss to sew stars and ^{1}/$_2$" dia. button to hat over gathers.
5. For hat brim, glue green felt piece around bottom edge of hat, overlapping ends at back.
6. Glue nose to head. Insert pins for eyes. Glue remaining buttons on front of snowman.
7. Glue one side of hook and loop fastener to top of jar lid. Glue remaining side to bottom of snowman head. Place head on jar lid.
8. For bow tie, gather blue felt piece at center. Wrap yellow felt piece around gathers for knot; glue to secure. Glue bow tie to neck.

CHRISTMAS PEARS AND CREAM PIE

*F*or a creamy, decadent treat, give luscious Pears and Cream Pie, which features a spiced filling nestled in a homemade pie crust. Topped with holly leaves and berries made of dough, the merry dessert is baked to flaky perfection! Present the delectable gift in a hand-punched pie pan that can be displayed for years to come.

PEARS AND CREAM PIE

CRUST

- 2 cups plus 2 tablespoons all-purpose flour
- 2 teaspoons sugar
- 1/4 teaspoon salt
- 3/4 cup chilled butter, cut into pieces
- 3 to 4 tablespoons cold water

FILLING

- 6 cups peeled, cored, and sliced Bosc pears (about 5 medium pears)
- 3/4 cup firmly packed brown sugar
- 3 tablespoons all-purpose flour
- 1/2 teaspoon ground cinnamon
- 1/4 teaspoon ground nutmeg
- 1/4 teaspoon salt
- 1/2 cup whipping cream
- 1 teaspoon rum flavoring
  Red and green liquid food coloring

For crust, trace holly leaf pattern, page 115, onto stencil plastic; cut out. Combine flour, sugar, and salt in a food processor. Add butter and pulse process until mixture resembles coarse meal. Add water and pulse process until mixture begins to form a ball and pulls away from

sides of bowl. Divide dough into 2 balls; flatten slightly. Wrap in plastic wrap and chill 30 minutes.

Preheat oven to 450 degrees. Between sheets of plastic wrap, roll each ball of dough into a 12-inch circle. Transfer 1 dough circle to a 9-inch pie pan with tin-punch design. Set aside remaining dough for top crust.

For filling, place pears in crust. In a medium bowl, combine next 5 ingredients. Stir in whipping cream and rum flavoring; spread over pears. Place top crust on filling. Use a sharp knife to trim edge of dough; save dough scraps for decorations. Roll out dough scraps. Use a sharp knife and pattern to cut out 9 leaves. Roll dough into 9 small balls for berries. Using food coloring and a small brush, paint leaves green and berries red; arrange on top of pie. Cut out

center of pie with a 1-inch round cookie cutter. Bake 10 minutes. Reduce temperature to 350 degrees; bake 30 to 40 minutes longer or until crust is lightly browned. Cool completely. Store in an airtight container in refrigerator.

Yield: about 8 servings

TIN-PUNCH PIE PAN

You will need tracing paper, 9" aluminum pie pan, removable tape, thick layer of newspaper, hammer, and an awl.

1. Trace pattern, page 115, onto tracing paper; cut out pattern along solid line.
2. Place pattern, right side up, in bottom of pan; tape in place. Place pan on newspaper. Being careful to not punch through pan, use hammer and awl to lightly punch pan at each dot on pattern. Remove pattern.

NUTTY NOËL

*T*hese Sugared Maple Walnuts are a sure way to spread sweet thoughts! A maple and brown sugar glaze with a hint of orange bakes into a candy-like coating. Give the tasty tidbits in woodsy cones accented with greenery for a rustic presentation.

SUGARED MAPLE WALNUTS

1 egg white
3 tablespoons maple syrup
$^1/_8$ teaspoon orange extract
4 cups walnut halves
$^1/_2$ cup firmly packed brown sugar
$^1/_2$ teaspoon salt

Preheat oven to 225 degrees. In a medium bowl, beat egg white until foamy. Beat in maple syrup and orange extract. Stir in walnut halves. Stir in brown sugar and salt. Spread walnuts on a lightly greased baking sheet. Bake 1 hour or until golden brown, stirring every 15 minutes. Cool on pan. Store in an airtight container.

Yield: about 5 cups walnuts

NUTTY GIFT

You will need a plastic bag to fit inside container, container with handle (we used a birch bark cone), yarn, jute twine, glue, and artificial greenery (we used holly leaves with berries).

1. Place plastic bag inside container. Place nuts in bag. Tie yarn and twine into a bow around gathers.
2. Glue greenery to handle.

"BEARY" MERRY CANDIES

*M*ake folks happy
during the hustle and bustle of
the holidays with Crispy
Peanut Butter Candies. Dry-
roasted peanuts and cocoa-
flavored crispy rice cereal add
crunch to each delectable
morsel. Ensure a festive
delivery by tucking the candies
in a "beary" cute brown paper
bag accented with a dapper
Christmas bow.

CRISPY PEANUT BUTTER CANDIES

- 16 ounces vanilla candy coating, chopped
- $^1/_2$ cup smooth peanut butter
- $1^1/_2$ cups dry-roasted peanuts
- 1 cup cocoa-flavored crispy rice cereal
- 1 cup miniature marshmallows

In top of a double boiler, melt candy coating over hot, not simmering, water. Stir in peanut butter until well blended. Remove from heat. Stir in peanuts, cereal, and marshmallows. Drop by rounded teaspoonfuls onto waxed paper. Let candy harden. Store in an airtight container.

Yield: about $7^1/_2$ dozen candies

BEAR FACE GIFT BAG

You will need tracing paper; tan, brown, and black craft foam; transfer paper; lunch-size brown paper bag; pink colored pencil; black permanent medium-point marker; glue; two $^1/_2$" dia. black buttons for eyes; stapler; 23" of $1^1/_2$"w red plaid wired ribbon; and a $1^1/_8$" dia. red button.

For gift tag, you will *also* need green paper, black permanent fine-point marker, and a $1^5/_8$" x $2^5/_8$" piece of cream paper.

1. Trace patterns, page 116, onto tracing paper; cut out. Use patterns to cut two outer ears from tan foam, two inner ears from brown foam, and one nose from black foam.
2. Use transfer paper to transfer face details to front of bag. Use pink colored pencil to add cheeks. Use medium-point marker to draw over transferred face details. Glue nose and black buttons to face.

3. Place gift in bag. Fold bag 2" to back. Staple fold at each corner to secure.
4. For each ear, glue one inner ear on one outer ear. Covering staples, glue ears to bag.
5. For bow tie, tie ribbon into a bow. Glue bow to front of bag; glue red button to knot of bow.
6. Use tag pattern to cut tag from green paper. Use fine-point marker to write "Have A Beary Merry Christmas!" on cream paper piece; glue to tag. Glue tag to bag.

COUNTRY CHRISTMAS TREES

*T*is the season for spreading good cheer to all your favorite folks! These charming Country Christmas Tree cookies are baked on sticks and "rooted" in excelsior-filled clay pots decorated with torn fabric and simple wooden ornaments. Brightly colored icing trims the trees with holiday flair.

COUNTRY CHRISTMAS TREES

COOKIES

- $1/2$ cup butter or margarine, softened
- $1/2$ cup firmly packed brown sugar
- $1/2$ cup molasses
- 1 egg
- 1 teaspoon vanilla extract
- $2^{1}/2$ cups all-purpose flour
- 1 teaspoon ground ginger
- 1 teaspoon ground cinnamon
- $1/4$ teaspoon ground nutmeg
- $1/4$ teaspoon ground cloves
- $1/4$ teaspoon salt
   Craft sticks

ICING

- $1^{1}/2$ cups sifted confectioners sugar
- 3 tablespoons vegetable shortening
- 2 to 3 teaspoons milk
- 1 teaspoon vanilla extract
   Red, yellow, and green paste food coloring

For cookies, trace tree pattern, page 116, onto stencil plastic; cut out. In a large bowl, cream butter and brown sugar until fluffy. Add molasses, egg, and vanilla; beat until smooth. In a medium bowl, combine flour, ginger, cinnamon, nutmeg, cloves, and salt. Add dry ingredients to

creamed mixture; stir until a soft dough forms. Divide dough in half. Wrap in plastic wrap and chill 2 hours.

Preheat oven to 350 degrees. On a lightly floured surface, use a floured rolling pin to roll out half of dough to $1/4$-inch thickness. Use pattern and a sharp knife to cut out cookies. Transfer to a greased baking sheet. Push a craft stick into bottom of each cookie. Bake 8 to 10 minutes or until edges are lightly browned. Cool cookies on baking sheet 2 minutes; transfer to a wire rack to cool

completely. Repeat with remaining dough.

For icing, combine confectioners sugar, shortening, milk, and vanilla in a small bowl; beat until smooth. Place $1/4$ cup icing in each of 2 small bowls; tint icing red and yellow. Tint remaining icing green. Transfer icing to pastry bags fitted with small round tips. Outline trees with green icing. Pipe small and large red or yellow dots on each tree. Let icing harden. Store in a single layer in an airtight container.

Yield: about 16 cookies

83

HEARTWARMING SNACKS

Glazed with an undeniably sweet coating, our Candied Mixed Nuts are a delicious way to enjoy an old snacking favorite. The tempting goodies are a joy to receive when they're packed in crimson boxes bearing your heartwarming messages.

CANDIED MIXED NUTS

- 5 cans (11½ ounces each) salted mixed nuts
- 1 cup sugar
- ½ cup butter or margarine
- ½ cup light corn syrup
- 2 teaspoons vanilla extract
- 1 teaspoon baking soda

Preheat oven to 200 degrees. Place nuts in a large greased roasting pan. In a heavy medium saucepan, combine sugar, butter, and corn syrup. Stirring constantly, cook over medium-low heat until sugar dissolves. Increase heat to medium and bring syrup to a boil. Cook, without stirring, 5 minutes. Remove from heat. Stir in vanilla and baking soda (mixture will foam). Pour syrup over nuts; stir until well coated. Bake 1 hour, stirring every 15 minutes. Spread on aluminum foil to cool. Store in an airtight container.

Yield: about 15½ cups nuts

HOLIDAY CONTAINERS

For each container, you will need a container at least 1⅜" high with lid (we used heart-shaped plastic containers), ⅝"w ribbon, glue, paint pen, decorative sticker, and a black permanent fine-point marker.

1. Measure around container; add ½". Cut a length of ribbon the determined measurement. Overlapping ends at top, glue ribbon around sides of container.

2. Use paint pen to write message along edge of lid. Apply sticker to center of lid top. Use marker to write message on sticker.

PERFECTLY PEACHY

*R*esting atop a layer of juicy peach slices, our Peachy Gingerbread takes on a unique flavor! Serve the squares warm from the oven, or cool them and package a perfectly pleasing gift. Wrap the pan of treats in colorful cellophane and tie it together with a crafty handmade tag.

PEACHY GINGERBREAD

    1 can (16 ounces) peach slices
         packed in juice
    1 package (14¹/₂ ounces)
         gingerbread mix
    1 egg
 ¹/₃ cup quick-cooking oats
 ¹/₄ cup firmly packed brown sugar
    3 tablespoons butter or margarine,
         softened

Preheat oven to 350 degrees. Drain juice from peaches into a 2-cup measuring cup. Add enough water to juice to measure amount of liquid needed on gingerbread mix package. In a medium bowl, combine gingerbread mix, juice mixture, and egg. Beat at low speed of an electric mixer 2 minutes. Place drained peaches in bottom of a lightly greased 8-inch square baking pan. Pour batter over peaches. In a small bowl, mix oats, brown sugar, and butter with a fork until well blended. Sprinkle over batter. Bake 43 to 48 minutes or until a toothpick inserted in center of gingerbread comes out clean. Cool in pan on a wire rack 20 minutes. Cut into 2-inch squares. Serve warm or cool completely.

Yield: about 16 servings

CHRISTMAS WRAP AND BOW

You will need 1 yd. each of 30"w red and green cellophane, 1¹/₄ yds. of 3"w wired ribbon, artificial poinsettia sprig, and white artificial twigs.

For gift tag, you will *also* need decorative-edge craft scissors, white paper, 1" x 1¹/₂" Christmas-motif sticker, black permanent fine-point marker, hole punch, and white embroidery floss.

1. Place cellophane pieces together on flat surface. Place pan of gingerbread at center of cellophane. Gather edges of cellophane over pan. Tie ribbon into a bow around gathers. Glue twigs and poinsettia sprig to knot of bow.

2. For gift tag, use craft scissors to cut a 1⁵/₈" x 3¹/₄" piece from white paper. Apply sticker to tag. Use marker to write message on tag. Punch hole in corner of tag. Thread floss through hole and tie to bow.

POP GOES THE SNOWMAN!

*T*his recipe is a fun, hands-on way to get kids involved in making homemade gifts. Our Popcorn Snowman is a cute decoration that's good to eat, too! His charming features and scarf are made from an assortment of candy pieces, and a top hat completes his ensemble.

POPCORN SNOWMAN

Mixture sets up quickly; have someone help you shape the snowman.

24	cups popped white popcorn
2	cups sugar
1	cup light corn syrup
1	tablespoon butter or margarine
2	teaspoons cream of tartar
3/4	teaspoon salt
1	teaspoon vanilla extract
1/2	teaspoon baking soda
	12-inch-long wooden skewer

Place popcorn in a large greased roasting pan. Butter sides of a heavy medium saucepan. Combine sugar, corn syrup, butter, cream of tartar, and salt in pan. Stirring constantly, cook over medium-high heat until mixture is fluid (about 5 minutes). Using a pastry brush dipped in hot water, wash down any sugar crystals on sides of pan. Attach a candy thermometer to pan, making sure thermometer does not touch bottom of pan. Cook, without stirring, until mixture reaches hard-ball stage (approximately 250 to 268 degrees). Test about 1/2 teaspoon mixture in ice water. Mixture will roll into a hard ball in ice water and will remain hard when removed from the water. Remove from heat and stir in vanilla and baking soda (mixture will foam). Pour mixture over popcorn; stir until coated. As soon as mixture is cool enough to handle, use greased hands to shape one 8-inch-diameter ball, one 6-inch-diameter ball, and one 4-inch-diameter ball; let cool. Stack balls on a plate from largest to smallest. Insert skewer through center of balls to secure.

Yield: one 13-inch-high snowman

POP THE SNOWMAN

You will need Popcorn Snowman (see recipe this page), toothpicks, candies to decorate snowman (we used black jelly beans for eyes and mouth, candy corn for nose, two cherry sours for buttons on body, and seven 27" lengths of red licorice laces for scarf), two artificial sprigs of greenery (we used holly sprigs with berries), glue, 12" length of 5/8"w grosgrain ribbon, 6" dia. black felt hat (including brim), tracing paper, green felt, two 10" wooden skewers, and two 9" lengths of red embroidery floss.

Remove toothpicks, skewers, greenery, and hat before eating.

1. Use toothpicks to attach candies for eyes, nose, mouth, and buttons to snowman. Tie licorice laces around neck. Tuck one greenery sprig behind scarf at side of neck.
2. Overlapping ends at one side, glue ribbon around hat for hatband; glue remaining greenery sprig over ends.
3. Trace mitten pattern, page 116, onto tracing paper. Use pattern to cut four mittens from felt. Trim skewer to desired arm length. For each arm, glue cut end of skewer between two mitten shapes. Tie one floss length into a bow around wrist of mitten. Insert skewers into sides of snowman.

CHEERY CHUTNEY

A fat-free treat that's especially delectable when accompanied by smooth cream cheese, our Pineapple-Mango Chutney makes a superb topper for crackers! Create a nice gift by filling a jar with the sauce and topping it with a padded fabric lid. A cross-stitched ornament is a lasting token to accompany the basket that carries your surprise.

PINEAPPLE-MANGO CHUTNEY

Chilled jars of mango slices can be found in the produce department.

- 2 tablespoons minced onion
- 1 clove garlic, minced
- 1 tablespoon olive oil
- 1 jar (26 ounces) sliced mango in light syrup, drained and coarsely chopped
- 2 jars (12 ounces each) pineapple preserves
- 1 cup golden raisins
- 1/2 cup orange juice
- 1/4 cup cider vinegar
- 1 teaspoon ground ginger
  Fat-free cream cheese and crackers to give

In a heavy medium saucepan, combine onion, garlic, and oil. Sauté over medium heat about 5 minutes or until vegetables are tender. Add mango, preserves, raisins, orange juice, vinegar, and ginger. Stirring frequently, cook over medium heat until mixture comes to a boil. Reduce heat to medium-low and simmer uncovered 15 minutes. Spoon chutney into heat-resistant jars; cover and cool to room temperature. Store in refrigerator.

Yield: about 5 cups chutney

DECORATED BASKET AND JAR LID

You will need embroidery floss (see color key, page 117), 6" square of White Aida (14 ct), 3¹/₂" dia. wooden frame, hot glue gun, artificial greenery (we used sprigs of pine and holly berries with leaves), a basket with handle (we used a 8¹/₂" x 12" divided basket), ⁵/₈"w satin ribbon, fabric for basket liner and jar lid insert, and a canning jar.

Refer to Cross Stitch and Embroidery Stitches, page 123, before beginning project.

1. Using three strands of floss for *Cross Stitch* and one strand for *Backstitch* and *French Knots*, center and stitch design, page 117, on Aida. Mount stitched piece in frame.
2. Glue frame to side of basket handle. Glue greenery to top of frame. Tie a length of ribbon into a bow; glue to top of frame.
3. Follow *Making a Basket Liner*, page 123, to make liner with a finished edge.
4. Follow *Jar Lid Finishing*, page 121, to cover jar lid. Tie ribbon into a bow around lid. Tuck greenery under knot of bow; glue to secure.

PEACHY DELIGHT

A blend of fat-free whipped topping and puréed peaches makes a tasty dessert that boasts lots of flavor — without all the fat! Crumbled vanilla creme cookies provide a crunchy topping, and a handmade card decorated with a charm-accented bow announces your gift with style.

FROZEN PEACH TORTE

- 1 package (7³/₄ ounces) low-fat vanilla creme sandwich cookies, crushed and divided (about 1³/₄ cups)
- 3 cans (16 ounces each) sliced peaches in juice, drained
- 1 cup sugar
- ¹/₂ teaspoon vanilla extract
- ¹/₂ teaspoon almond extract
- 2 cups fat-free frozen whipped topping, thawed

Reserving ¹/₃ cup cookie crumbs, press remaining crumbs into bottom of an ungreased 9-inch springform pan. Reserve 12 peach slices to garnish. Process remaining peaches, sugar, and extracts in a food processor until smooth. Transfer mixture to a medium bowl. Fold in whipped topping. Pour mixture over crust. Cover and freeze overnight.

To serve, sprinkle reserved cookie crumbs over top and garnish with reserved peach slices.

Yield: 12 servings

1 serving (1 slice): 213 calories, 1.8 grams fat, 1.4 grams protein, 46.7 grams carbohydrates

GIFT CARD

You will need a 3¹/₂" x 5³/₄" piece of handmade paper, black permanent fine-point marker, gold paint pen, glue, 6" length of 2"w sheer ribbon, floral wire, wire cutters, and a gold charm.

1. For card, matching short ends, fold paper piece in half.
2. With fold at top, lightly draw a line ¹/₈" inside all edges on front of card. Use marker to draw a wavy line along drawn line. Use paint pen to paint edges outside wavy line.
3. For bow, overlapping ends ¹/₂", glue ribbon ends together. With overlapped ends at center back, pinch ribbon at center to form two loops; wrap wire around gathers. Trim wire ends close to back of bow. Glue charm to front of bow, covering wire. Glue bow to center of card.
4. Use paint pen to write message on card.

CHEESY PARTY CRACKERS

*Z*esty herbs and cheese make these simple oyster crackers a real party hit! When you fill napkin-decorated gift bags with the crispy crackers and clip them with handmade felt stocking magnets, you'll have great favors to pass out to departing guests.

CHEESY HERB CRACKERS

- 2 packages (10 ounces each) oyster crackers
- 1/2 cup vegetable oil
- 1/4 cup grated Parmesan cheese
- 1 package (1 1/4 ounces) cheese sauce mix
- 3/4 teaspoon garlic powder
- 1/2 teaspoon ground oregano
- 1/2 teaspoon celery seed
- 1/2 teaspoon salt
- 1/8 teaspoon ground red pepper

Preheat oven to 300 degrees. Place oyster crackers in a large roasting pan. In a small bowl, combine oil, Parmesan cheese, cheese sauce mix, garlic powder, oregano, celery seed, salt, and red pepper; whisk until blended. Pour oil mixture over crackers; stir until well coated. Bake 15 minutes, stirring every 5 minutes. Spread on aluminum foil to cool. Store in an airtight container.

Yield: about 12 cups snack mix

GIFT BAGS WITH STOCKING MAGNETS

For each bag, you will need a lunch-size white paper bag, printed paper napkin, and spray adhesive.

For each stocking magnet, you will *also* need tracing paper; white felt for cuff; green and red felt for stocking; glue; pinking shears; three 6mm jingle bells; wooden spring-type clothespin; 1 3/4" length of 3/8"w magnetic strip; and several lengths of white, green, and red curling ribbon.

Instructions are for making a magnet with a green stocking. For a magnet with a red stocking, reverse green and red felt.

1. For bag, unfold and press napkin. Separate napkin into layers.
2. Apply spray adhesive to wrong side of printed napkin layer; glue to front of bag. Trim napkin even with edges of bag.

3. For magnet, trace stocking and cuff patterns, page 117, onto tracing paper. Use patterns to cut stocking from green felt and cuff from white felt.
4. Glue stocking to red felt. Trim red felt even with stocking top. Using pinking shears and leaving a 1/4" red felt border along sides and bottom of stocking, cut out stocking. Glue cuff to stocking top. Glue one bell to each point of cuff.
5. Glue stocking to clothespin. Glue magnetic strip to opposite side of clothespin.
6. Tie several lengths of curling ribbon together; glue knot inside clothespin clasp. Curl ends of ribbon. Place gift in bag. Fold bag 2" to front. Use clothespin to secure.

"MEOW-Y" CHRISTMAS!

*F*urry *friends deserve a "Meow-y" Christmas, too! Stitch festive stockings from colorful felt, then fill them with a cat's favorite treat — catnip! Fun handmade gift tags are a "purr-fect" finish for this creative offering.*

CATNIP STOCKINGS

For each stocking, you will need tracing paper; two 5" x 7" pieces of red or green felt; red, green, and white felt scraps; white embroidery floss; dried catnip; and an 8" length of 1/4"w red grosgrain ribbon.

For gift tag, you will *also* need a black permanent fine-point marker, white paper, glue, green paper, decorative-edge craft scissors, and a hole punch.

Instructions are for making a red stocking. For a green stocking, reverse red and green felt.

1. Trace stocking, cuff, large snowflake, medium snowflake, and small snowflake patterns, page 118, onto tracing paper; cut out. Draw around stocking pattern on one 5" x 7" red felt piece; do not cut out. Cut one cuff from white felt and one small snowflake from red felt. Use pinking shears to cut one each medium and large snowflake from green felt and one medium snowflake from white felt.
2. Arrange snowflakes on drawn stocking. Use three strands of floss to work three *Straight Stitches,* page 123, in center of each snowflake, crisscrossing stitches at each center and stitching through all layers.
3. Place two felt pieces together with decorated piece on top. Leaving top open,

stitch along drawn line. Cut out stocking along drawn line at top and 1/4" outside sewn line.
4. Fill stocking with catnip.
5. Center long straight edge of cuff along top edge of stocking. Stitching through all layers, stitch along top edge of stocking.
6. Tie ribbon into a bow. Glue to stocking top.

7. For gift tag, use marker to write "Meow-y Christmas!" on white paper; cut out. Glue tag to green paper. Use craft scissors to cut out tag. Punch hole in corner of tag. Loop a length of floss through hole and tie ends together to make hanger.

FRUITY FRIENDSHIP BASKET

*R*efreshing Friendship Sauce makes a scrumptious addition to our tasty muffins! Your friends can use the jar of sauce you include in the gift basket to make more delicious muffins or as a topping for ice cream or pound cake. They can even use the sauce to start a batch of their own. What a wonderfully versatile recipe!

FRIENDSHIP FRUIT SAUCE

YEAST STARTER

  1 cup sugar
  2 packages dry yeast
  1 can (15¼ ounces) pineapple chunks in heavy syrup

FRUIT SAUCE

  1 recipe yeast starter
  1 can (15¼ ounces) pineapple chunks in heavy syrup
  4 cups sugar, divided
  1 can (16 ounces) sliced peaches in syrup
  1 can (14 ounces) apricot halves in syrup, cut in half
  1 jar (10 ounces) maraschino cherries

For yeast starter, combine sugar, yeast, and undrained pineapple in a 1-quart nonmetal container with a loose-fitting lid. Stir several times during first day to make sure sugar and yeast dissolve. Let mixture stand 2 weeks at room temperature; stir daily.

For fruit sauce, place yeast starter in a 1-gallon nonmetal container with a loose-fitting lid. Add undrained pineapple and 1 cup sugar. Let fruit mixture stand 1 week at room temperature; stir daily.

For week 2, add undrained peaches and 1 cup sugar; stir daily.

For week 3, add undrained apricot pieces and 1 cup sugar; stir daily.

For week 4, add undrained cherries and remaining 1 cup sugar; stir daily.

At end of fourth week, let mixture stand 3 days longer at room temperature; stir daily. Fruit sauce is now ready to use. Serve over ice cream, pound cake, or use in Friendship Fruit Muffins (recipe follows). Reserve at least 1½ cups fruit sauce to start a new batch of sauce.

To replenish fruit sauce, add 1 can undrained fruit (alternating types of fruit) and 1 cup sugar every week. Stir mixture daily. Let mixture stand 3 days at room temperature before using.

For each gift, give 1½ cups fruit sauce, replenishing instructions, and muffin recipe.

Yield: about 10 cups fruit sauce

FRIENDSHIP FRUIT MUFFINS

    Vegetable cooking spray
  1 cup drained fruit from Friendship Fruit Sauce
  ½ cup syrup from Friendship Fruit Sauce
  1 cup sugar, divided
  ½ teaspoon ground cinnamon
  1 cup butter, melted
  1 container (8 ounces) sour cream at room temperature
  2 cups self-rising flour

Preheat oven to 350 degrees. Line a muffin pan with paper muffin cups. Spray cups with cooking spray. In a small bowl, combine fruit, syrup, ½ cup sugar, and cinnamon. In a medium bowl, combine melted butter and sour cream. Add flour and remaining ½ cup sugar to sour cream mixture; stir just until moistened. Spoon 2 tablespoons batter into prepared muffin cups. Spoon 1 tablespoon fruit mixture over batter. Bake 30 to 35 minutes or until golden brown. Serve warm.

Yield: about 1½ dozen muffins

WHITE POINSETTIA BASKET

You will need gold spray paint, basket with handle (we used a 9½" dia. basket), fabric for basket liner, floral wire, wire cutters, artificial greenery (we used one 8" and one 5" white poinsettia with leaves and sprigs of ivy), 37" length of gold decorative cord with tassels on each end, and a glass jar with a knobbed lid.

1. Spray paint basket gold.
2. Follow *Making a Basket Liner*, page 123, to make liner with a finished edge.
3. Use wire to attach greenery to basket handle.
4. Tie gold cord into a bow around knob on lid.

SUGARPLUM COOKIES

*R*ight out of a Christmas Eve dream, our Sugarplum Cookies are enough to satisfy any sweet tooth! Decorated with swirled icing to resemble lollipops, store-bought cookies become divine confections. Keep these delectable treats in a fabric-covered bag accented with matching candy ornaments.

SUGARPLUM COOKIES

    4 cups sifted confectioners sugar
3¹/₂ to 4 tablespoons water
    1 tablespoon light corn syrup
    1 teaspoon vanilla extract
       Green and red paste food coloring
    1 package (11 ounces) firm sugar
       cookies (about 2 inches in
       diameter)

In a medium bowl, combine confectioners sugar, water, corn syrup, and vanilla; beat until smooth. Transfer about ¹/₂ cup icing into each of 3 small bowls. Tint green and red, leaving remaining icing white. Spoon each icing into a pastry bag fitted with a small round tip. Working with 3 cookies at a time, outline and fill in tops of cookies with a thin layer of green or red icing. While icing is still wet, pipe white icing onto cookies in a spiral design. Place on a wire rack to let icing harden. Store in an airtight container.

Yield: about 2 dozen cookies

SUGARPLUM GIFT BAG

You will need a white paper gift bag (we used a 6" x 11" bag), paper-backed fusible web, fabric, 1"w grosgrain ribbon, glue, and two lollipop ornaments.

1. Draw around front of bag on paper side of web. Fuse web to wrong side of fabric; cut out along drawn lines. Fuse fabric piece to front of bag.
2. Place cookies in bag.
3. Fold top of bag 2¹/₄" to front; glue to secure.
4. Measure width of bag; add 1". Cut a length of ribbon the determined measurement.
5. Glue ribbon across front of flap. Fold ribbon ends to back of flap; glue in place.
6. If necessary, remove hanging loops from ornaments. Glue ornaments to bag.

STRESS-FREE APPLE CRISP

*A*n apple a day keeps the doctor away, and an Apple Crisp Kit will keep the holiday stress at bay! Your friends can toss this simple dessert together in minutes using the crumbly homemade topping and purchased apple pie filling. Create a sponge-painted holly wreath bag to present the tasty kit, and you'll have a super gift idea for a special family.

APPLE CRISP KIT

2	cups all-purpose flour
1	cup firmly packed brown sugar
1	cup old-fashioned oats
1/2	teaspoon ground cinnamon
1/2	teaspoon salt
1/4	teaspoon ground nutmeg
1	cup chilled butter or margarine
1	cup chopped pecans
4	cans (21 ounces each) apple pie filling to give

In a large bowl, combine flour, brown sugar, oats, cinnamon, salt, and nutmeg. Using a pastry blender or 2 knives, cut in butter until mixture resembles coarse meal. Stir in pecans. Divide topping into 2 resealable plastic bags; store in refrigerator. Give each bag of topping with 2 cans apple pie filling and serving instructions.

Yield: about 7 cups topping

To serve: Spread 2 cans apple pie filling in a lightly greased 9 x 13-inch baking dish. Sprinkle topping over apples. Bake in a 400-degree oven 19 to 21 minutes or until filling bubbles and topping is golden brown. Serve warm.

Yield: about 12 servings

HOLLY WREATH GIFT BAG

You will need tracing paper, compressed craft sponge, green and dark green acrylic paint, 10" x 13" red gift bag, black permanent fine-point marker, 3/8" to 1/2" dia. white buttons, glue, and a 28" length of 1 1/2"w wired ribbon.

1. Trace leaf pattern, page 119, onto tracing paper; cut out. Use pattern to cut leaf from sponge.

2. Follow *Sponge Painting*, page 122, to paint green and dark green leaves in a wreath design on front of bag. Use marker to outline and add detail lines to leaves.
3. For each cluster of berries, glue three buttons to wreath.
4. Tie ribbon length into a bow. Glue bow to top of wreath.

FESTIVE CHOCOLATE ROCKS

*G*ive all your friends the rich flavor of fudge in a long-lasting hard candy. Pack the bite-size Chocolate Rocks in unique bags constructed of paper twist and tie the bags with shiny mesh bows. Add evergreen motifs and sparkling acrylic jewels for a holiday finish.

CHOCOLATE ROCKS

- 2   cups sugar
- 1   cup light corn syrup
- 1/2   cup cocoa
- 1/2   cup water
- 1/8   teaspoon salt
- 1   tablespoon butter or margarine
- 1   teaspoon vanilla extract

Line a 9 x 13-inch baking pan with aluminum foil, extending foil over ends of pan; grease foil. Butter sides of a heavy large saucepan. Combine sugar, corn syrup, cocoa, water, and salt in pan. Stirring constantly, cook over medium-low heat until sugar dissolves. Using a pastry brush dipped in hot water, wash down any sugar crystals on sides of pan. Attach a candy thermometer to pan, making sure thermometer does not touch bottom of pan. Increase heat to medium and bring to a boil. Cook, without stirring, until mixture reaches soft-crack stage (approximately 270 to 290 degrees). Test about 1/2 teaspoon mixture in ice water. Mixture will form hard threads in ice water but will soften when removed from the water. Remove from heat and stir in butter and vanilla. Pour into prepared pan. Let candy harden. Use ends of foil to

lift candy from pan. Break into pieces. Store in an airtight container.

Yield: about 1 1/4 pounds candy

PAPER TWIST BAGS

For each bag, you will need 16" length of red gingham paper twist (4 1/2"w untwisted), glue, pinking shears, 13" length of 1 1/2"w green mesh ribbon, tracing paper, green construction paper, and three 7mm red acrylic jewels.

1. Matching short ends, fold paper twist piece in half; glue long edges together. Trim open end with pinking shears.
2. Trace tree pattern, page 119, onto tracing paper. Use pattern to cut tree from green paper. Glue tree to front of bag. Glue jewels to tree.
3. Place candy in bag. Knot ribbon around top of bag.

WINE AND CHEESE BASKET

*N*eatly packaged *for two in a holly-trimmed basket, a gift of Cranberry Wine and Cheese Balls brings a classic taste of the holidays to a super couple. Etched wine glasses and a pretty bottle serve up the refreshing spirit, while cheeses blended with marinated cranberries make a delicious topper for crackers.*

CRANBERRY WINE

- 1 package (6 ounces) sweetened dried cranberries
- ¹/₂ cup water
- 1 bottle (750 ml) white wine

For wine, combine cranberries and water in a small saucepan over medium heat. Bring to a boil; boil 1 minute. Remove from heat and cool. In a half-gallon container, combine cranberry mixture and wine. Cover and chill 3 days.

Strain wine (we used a paper coffee filter), reserving cranberries for Cranberry Cheese Balls. Return wine to wine bottle; cork and store in refrigerator. *Yield:* about 3¹/₂ cups wine

CRANBERRY CHEESE BALLS

- 2 packages (8 ounces each) cream cheese, softened
- 2 cups (8 ounces) shredded sharp Cheddar cheese
- 1 cup reserved cranberries from Cranberry Wine, chopped
- 1¹/₂ cups chopped pecans, toasted, coarsely ground, and divided
    Crackers to give

In a large bowl, beat cheeses until well blended. Stir in cranberries and ¹/₄ cup pecans. Shape into 2 balls; roll in remaining pecans. Wrap in plastic wrap and store in refrigerator. Give with crackers.

Yield: 2 cheese balls (about 2 cups each)

FESTIVE STEMWARE AND BASKET

You will need wine glasses (we used glasses with a 2³/₄" dia. base), self-adhesive stars, glass etching cream, rubber gloves, 42" length of holly berry garland, 10" square basket with handle, glue, 1³/₈ yds. of 1¹/₄"w wired ribbon, and Christmas-motif fabric for basket liner.

1. For each glass, apply stars to outside of glass and top of base as desired.
2. Follow manufacturer's instructions to apply etching cream to outside of glass and top of base.
3. Remove etching cream and stars.
4. Arrange garland around rim of basket; glue in place.
5. Tie ribbon into a bow around handle. Arrange streamers as desired.
6. Use fabric for basket liner and follow *Making a Basket Liner*, page 123, to make liner with a finished edge. Place liner in basket. Place glasses and gifts in basket.

GIFT-BOXED CAKE

Who says you can't have your cake and eat it, too? Our Orange Marmalade Cake combines the citrusy punch of marmalade with the nutty crunch of pecans to make a truly tempting delicacy. A rich cream cheese icing blankets the cake for an unforgettable taste. The dessert will be perfect for gift-giving when you pack it in a covered cake box topped with a bow.

ORANGE MARMALADE CAKE

You will need one 18-ounce jar of marmalade for cake and filling.

CAKE

- 3/4 cup butter or margarine, softened
- 1 cup sugar
- 3 eggs
- 1 teaspoon vanilla extract
- 1 cup orange marmalade
- 2 1/2 cups all-purpose flour
- 1 teaspoon baking soda
- 1/8 teaspoon salt
- 1/2 cup buttermilk

FILLING

- 1/2 cup orange marmalade
- 1 cup chopped pecans
- 1 cup flaked coconut

ICING

- 1 package (8 ounces) cream cheese, softened
- 1/2 cup butter or margarine, softened
- 1 teaspoon vanilla extract
- 1 package (16 ounces) confectioners sugar, sifted

Preheat oven to 350 degrees. For cake, line bottoms of two 9-inch round cake pans with waxed paper. Grease waxed paper and sides of pans. In a large bowl, cream butter and sugar until fluffy. Add eggs and vanilla; beat until smooth. Beat in marmalade. In a medium bowl, combine flour, baking soda, and salt. Alternately beat dry ingredients and buttermilk into creamed mixture, beating until well blended. Spoon batter into prepared pans. Bake 30 to 35 minutes or until a toothpick inserted in center of cake comes out clean. Cool in pans 10 minutes. Remove from pans and cool completely on a wire rack.

For filling, melt marmalade in a medium saucepan over medium-low heat. Remove from heat. Stir in pecans and coconut. Split cake layers in half horizontally. Spread filling between layers. Place cake in an airtight container and chill 1 hour.

For icing, beat cream cheese and butter in a medium bowl until fluffy. Beat in vanilla. Gradually add confectioners sugar; beat until smooth. Spread icing over top and sides of cake. Store in an airtight container in refrigerator.

Yield: about 12 servings

COVERED CAKE BOX

You will need a 10" square x 5 1/2"h cake box, wrapping paper, spray adhesive, craft knife and cutting mat, one 1 yd. and one 3 yd. length of 1 7/8"w wired ribbon, and a 6" length of floral wire.

1. Unfold box. Cut a piece of wrapping paper 1" larger on all sides than unfolded box. Place wrapping paper wrong side up on a flat surface.
2. Apply spray adhesive to outside of entire box. Center unfolded box adhesive side down on paper; press firmly to secure.
3. Use craft knife to cut paper even with edges of box. If box has slits, use craft knife to cut through slits from inside of box. Reassemble box.
4. Place cake in box.
5. Twisting ribbon at bottom of box, wrap 3 yd. ribbon length around box and tie ends into a bow with two 8" loops and two 5 1/2" streamers. Using 1 yd. ribbon length, follow *Making a Bow*, page 121, to make a second bow with two 8" loops and two 5 1/2" streamers. Use wire at back to attach second bow to knot of first bow.

"Bee" Merry!

*A*waken the senses with refreshing Lemon-Ginger-Honey Jelly! A cool and inviting topper for biscuits, bread, and more, our out-of-the-ordinary jelly is a super surprise when it comes in a "Bee Merry" bag with a crafty Santa bee attached.

Lemon-Ginger-Honey Jelly

- 2 cups sugar
- 1¼ cups water
- ¾ cup freshly squeezed lemon juice (about 4 lemons)
- 2 tablespoons finely chopped crystallized ginger
- 2 cups honey
- 1 pouch (3 ounces) liquid fruit pectin

In a large Dutch oven, combine sugar, water, lemon juice, and ginger. Stirring constantly over high heat, bring mixture to a rolling boil. Stir in honey and liquid pectin. Stirring constantly, bring to a rolling boil again and boil 1 minute. Remove from heat; skim off foam. Pour jelly into heat-resistant jars; cover and cool to room temperature. Store in refrigerator.

Yield: about 5¼ cups jelly

"Bee Merry" Canvas Bag

You will need tracing paper, transfer paper, canvas bag, black permanent medium-point marker, yellow paper, red and white felt, black permanent broad-tip marker, black chenille stem, craft glue, 1" dia. black button, 8mm white pom-pom, and a 1½" x 3½" wooden heart for wings.

For jar lid insert you will *also* need one extra flat part of jar lid for pattern, cardboard, batting, and desired fabric.

1. Trace patterns, page 118, onto tracing paper. Use transfer paper to transfer words to bag. Use medium-point marker to draw over transferred lines.
2. Cut out body, hat, and hat brim. Use patterns to cut body from yellow paper, hat from red felt, and hat brim from white felt.
3. Use broad-tip marker to draw ¼"w stripes ¼" apart on body.

4. For head, cut a 6" length from chenille stem. Bend stem in half and curl ends. Glue center of stem to back of button. Glue hat brim and pom-pom to hat. Glue hat to head.
5. For wings, use medium-point marker to draw a curved dashed line along center of wooden heart.
6. Glue body and head to wings. Glue bee to bag.
7. Refer to *Jar Lid Finishing*, page 121, to cover jar lid.

100

CREAMY POTATO SOUP

A full-bodied blend of hearty ingredients, our Creamy Potato Soup will warm even the coldest tummies! Perfect for dinner in front of a roaring fire, this quick heat-and-eat meal can be served up in no time. The recipe makes plenty to go around, so you can present the steamy offering with a cute snowman pot holder that will remind your friends of the gift long after the soup is gone.

CREAMY POTATO SOUP

    1 package (26 ounces) frozen hash
         brown potatoes
 1¹/₂ cups frozen chopped onions
    2 cans (14¹/₂ ounces each) chicken
         broth
    2 cups water
    2 cups milk
    1 can (10³/₄ ounces) Cheddar cheese
         soup
    1 can (10³/₄ ounces) cream of celery
         soup
    1 can (10³/₄ ounces) cream of
         chicken-mushroom soup
 ³/₄ teaspoon ground white pepper
 ¹/₄ teaspoon dried thyme leaves

In a large Dutch oven, combine potatoes, onions, chicken broth, and water. Bring to a boil over high heat. Reduce heat to medium-low; cover and simmer 30 minutes. Stir in milk, soups, white pepper, and thyme. Stirring frequently, cook 15 minutes or until soups are blended and mixture is heated through. Serve warm. Store in an airtight container in refrigerator.

Yield: about 13 cups soup

SNOWMAN POT HOLDER

You will need tracing paper; transfer paper; 9" square white pot holder; white, orange, dark orange, red, and black acrylic paint; and paintbrushes.

Refer to Painting Techniques, page 122, for painting tips.

1. Trace snowman face pattern, page 119, onto tracing paper. Use transfer paper to lightly transfer design to right side of pot holder.
2. Paint eyes and mouth black, nose orange, and cheeks red. Use dark orange paint to add shading and detail lines to nose. Use white paint to add highlight to each eye.

CHIPS WITH A TWIST

These crunchy snacks have a delicious twist! Our Spicy Sweet Potato Chips are tossed in a marinade and baked until they're crisp. Pack them in a fabric-lined basket tied with ribbon and a jingle bell for a creative holiday surprise.

SPICY SWEET POTATO CHIPS

Chips can be dried in oven or dehydrator.

- $1/2$ cup vegetable oil
- $1/4$ cup minced fresh cilantro
- 2 tablespoons ground cumin
- 2 teaspoons garlic powder
- 2 teaspoons salt
- 1 teaspoon ground red pepper
- 4 large fresh sweet potatoes

If using a dehydrator, follow manufacturer's instructions for drying. If using an oven, preheat to 140 degrees (use an oven thermometer to monitor temperature). In a large bowl, combine oil, cilantro, cumin, garlic powder, salt, and red pepper. Cut unpeeled sweet potatoes into $1/8$-inch slices (we used a mandolin slicer). Toss slices in marinade until well coated. Place slices on wire cooling racks in oven or on dehydrator racks. Dry about 17 hours, testing for doneness by cooling a chip and testing for crispness. Let chips cool. Store in an airtight container.
Yield: about 7 cups potato chips

BASKET WITH LINER AND BOW

You will need glue, artificial greenery (we used pine sprigs, berries, and a small pinecone), basket with handle (we used a

$5^1/_2$" x $14^1/_2$" basket), fabric for liner and bow, one 6" and one 16" length of $1/4$"w satin ribbon, and a 1" dia. jingle bell.

1. Glue greenery to basket handle.
2. Tear a $1^3/_4$" x 20" strip of fabric. Tie strip into a bow around greenery and handle.
3. Tie 16" ribbon length into a bow around center of 6" ribbon length. Glue ribbon bow and bell to knot of fabric bow.
4. For basket liner, follow *Making a Basket Liner*, page 123, to make liner with an unfinished edge.

PARTY POPCORN

*S*erve quick-to-make *Ranch-Style Popcorn at your holiday get-together, and watch it disappear! The crunchy baked snack is covered with a buttery dressing mix for a unique taste treat. At the end of the party, favor guests with fun take-home bags of popcorn. The cute sacks are easy to decorate using fused-on appliqués and matching gift tags.*

RANCH-STYLE POPCORN

  20 cups popped popcorn
  ½ cup butter or margarine, melted
   2 packages (0.4 ounce each)
        ranch-style salad dressing mix

Preheat oven to 300 degrees. Place popcorn in a large roasting pan. In a small bowl, combine melted butter and salad dressing mix; whisk until well blended. Pour mixture over popcorn; stir until well coated. Bake 20 minutes, stirring after 10 minutes. Spread on aluminum foil to cool. Store in an airtight container.

Yield: about 12 cups popcorn

STOCKING APPLIQUÉ BAGS

For each bag, you will need paper-backed fusible web, red and green fabric scraps for appliqués, kraft paper, black permanent medium-point marker, serrated-edge craft scissors, glue, and a lunch-size gift bag.

For gift tag, you will *also* need a 9" length of ivory embroidery floss and a large button.

1. Use patterns, page 120, and follow *Making Appliqués,* page 122, to make one stocking appliqué from red fabric; do not remove paper backing. Make one each of heel, toe, and 2⅛" x 4⅛" tag appliqués from green fabric.

2. Arrange heel and toe on stocking; fuse in place. Remove paper backing and fuse stocking to kraft paper. Use marker to draw "stitches" around stocking. Cutting close to stitches, use craft scissors to cut

out stocking. Glue stocking to front of bag.

3. Fuse tag appliqué to kraft paper. Leaving a narrow kraft paper border, cut out tag. Cut a 1⅛" x 3⅜" piece of kraft paper; glue to center of tag. Use marker to write message on tag.

4. Thread floss through holes in button and tie into a bow at front. Glue button to tag; glue tag to bag.

Using our fast-to-finish recipe, you can make these treats and be out of the kitchen in a flash! Haystacks are concocted of a few basic ingredients, and one batch makes plenty for sharing. Present the chocolaty goodies in papier-mâché "book" boxes covered with pretty holiday fabrics. What a great way to wish bookworms a merry Christmas!

HAYSTACKS

These candies set up quickly, so get a friend to help drop them.

    1 container (1 pound, 7 ounces)
          Spanish-style peanuts
    1 container (7 ounces) potato sticks
   12 ounces chocolate candy coating,
          chopped
    1 package (6 ounces) semisweet
          chocolate chips
    1 cup peanut butter chips
  1/4 cup smooth peanut butter

Combine peanuts and potato sticks in a large bowl. In a large microwave-safe bowl, combine candy coating, chocolate chips, peanut butter chips, and peanut butter. Microwave on medium-high power (80%) about 3 minutes or until mixture melts, stirring after each minute. Pour over peanut mixture; stir until well coated. Quickly drop tablespoonfuls of mixture onto baking sheets lined with waxed paper; chill until firm. Store in an airtight container in refrigerator.

Yield: about 7 1/2 dozen candies

BOOK BOX

You will need a 7" x 9" papier-mâché book-shaped box, print fabric to cover inside and outside of book and a coordinating fabric to cover spine, 3/4 yd. of 1 3/8"w sheer ribbon, artificial greenery (we used a sprig of holly leaves with berries), ecru acrylic paint, glossy wood-tone spray, brown permanent fine-point marker, ruler, spray adhesive, and glue.

Throughout these instructions, we refer to the book box as "book."

Apply spray adhesive to wrong sides of all fabric pieces before applying to book.

1. From print fabric, cut an 11" x 17 1/2" piece for outside cover, a 2" x 21" piece for inside front and side edges, and an 8 1/4" x 14 1/2" for inside of book. From coordinating fabric, cut a 4" x 11" piece for spine.
2. Allowing to dry after each application, paint "pages" ecru, then lightly spray with wood-tone spray. Use marker and ruler to draw lines for "pages."
3. To cover outside of book, place book on wrong side of fabric with bottom edge of book 1/4" from one short edge of fabric. Press fabric around book. Fold fabric corners diagonally over book

corners; press edges of fabric over edges of book.
4. For spine, center spine of book on wrong side of fabric piece (Fig. 1). Press fabric in place around book. Press excess fabric over edges of book at top and bottom; trim to fit if necessary.

Fig. 1

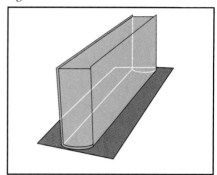

5. For lining, press fabric strip for inside edges onto inside front and sides of book. Press remaining fabric piece onto inside of lid, spine, and bottom of book (Fig. 2).

Fig. 2

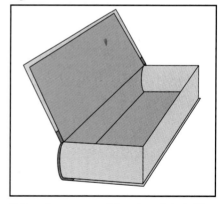

6. For closure, cut ribbon length in half. Glue one end of one ribbon length 1/2" from opening edge of center book front; glue one end of remaining length 1/2" from bottom edge of center book back. Glue greenery to front of book covering ribbon end. Tie ribbons into a bow.

"FAMILY RECIPES" GIFT SET
(page 7)

ELF BAG
(page 8)

Nose

Ear

CROSS STITCH JAR LID
(page 14)

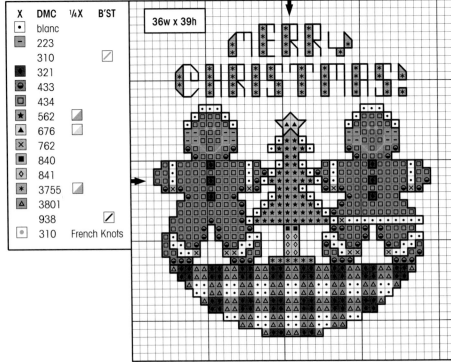

X	DMC	¼X	B'ST
⊡	blanc		
⊟	223		
	310		◺
◼	321		
◕	433		
▢	434		
★	562	◪	
▲	676	◪	
⊠	762		
◼	840		
◇	841		
✳	3755	◪	
◮	3801		
	938		◹
⊙	310	French Knots	

36w x 39h

MERRY CHRISTMAS

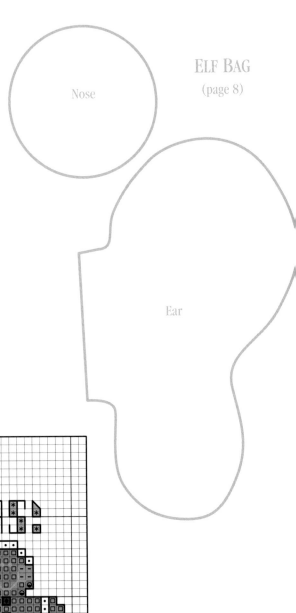

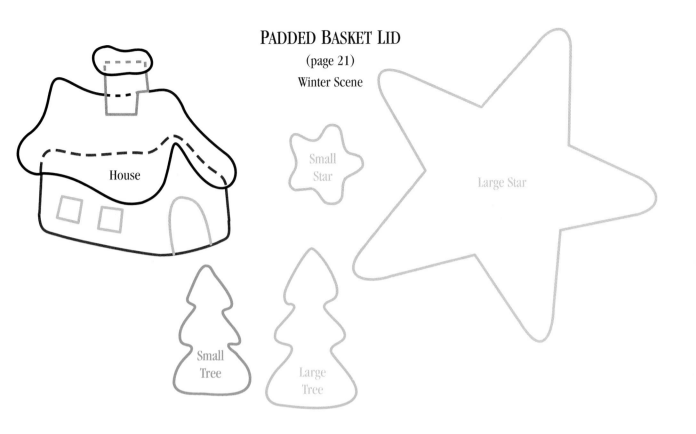

PADDED BASKET LID

(page 21)

Winter Scene

House

Small Star

Large Star

Small Tree

Large Tree

SOUP MIX BAGS

(page 57)

BEANS

PASTA

To serve: Rinse and sort dried beans. In a large Dutch oven, combine beans and 12 cups water. Cover and bring to a boil over medium-high heat. Reduce heat to medium-low and cook $1^1/_4$ hours. Stir in seasoning mix, pasta, 2 cans ($14^1/_2$ ounces each) diced tomatoes, and 1 can (8 ounces) tomato sauce. Cover and simmer 30 minutes or until beans are tender. Serve warm.

PATTERNS (continued)

BUSY ELF CANS
(page 19)

DECORATED MINI BASKET
(page 18)

Small Star

Large Star

Tree Top

Tree Center

A TRIO OF BOXES
(page 51)

Leaf

Nose

Tree Bottom

Trunk

Hat

FABRIC-TRIMMED BAG
(page 28)

MUSTARD PRETZEL MIX

SPICE MUG MATS IN GIFT BASKET
(page 33)

Leaf

Stem

Apple

STRING-OF-LIGHTS GIFT CARD
(page 41)

Bulb

APPLIQUÉD CANDY TIN
(page 34)

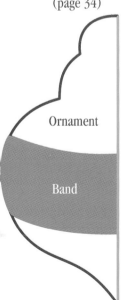

Ornament

Band

JINGLE DOG DISH
(page 35)

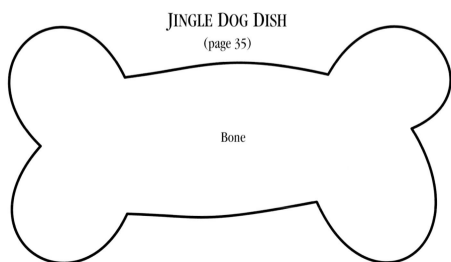

Bone

PATTERNS (continued)

DECORATED JAR LIDS

(page 36)

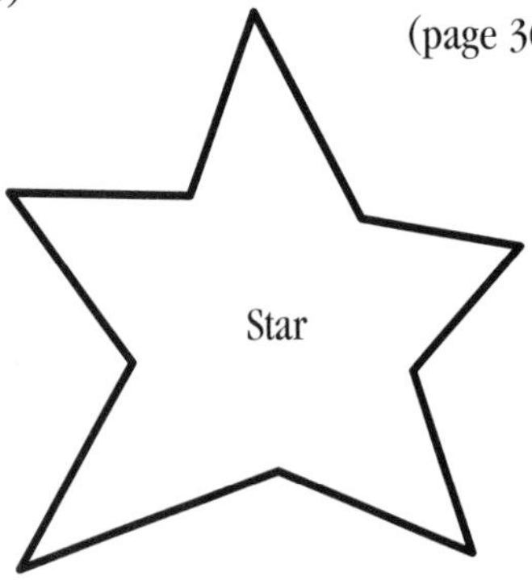
Star

SANTA BAG

(page 61)

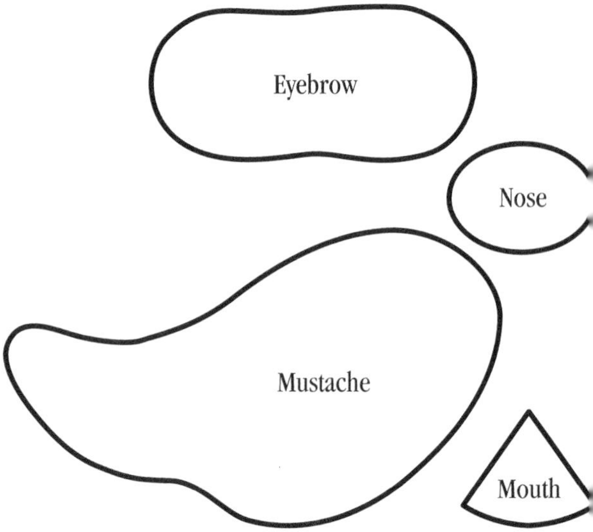
Eyebrow
Nose
Mustache
Mouth

BUTTON TREE PIN

(page 49)

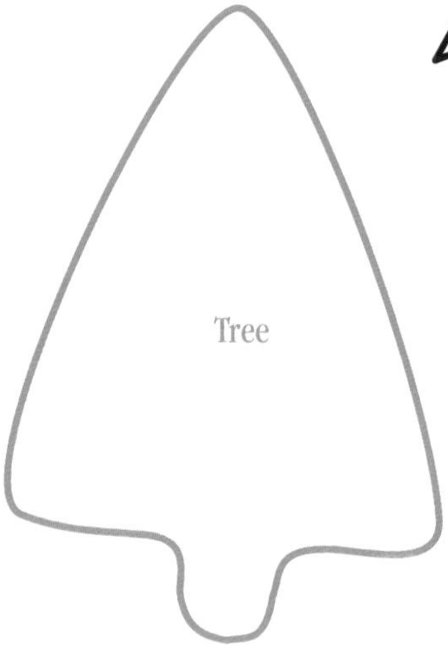
Tree

"SEASON'S GREETINGS" BREADCOVER

(page 48)

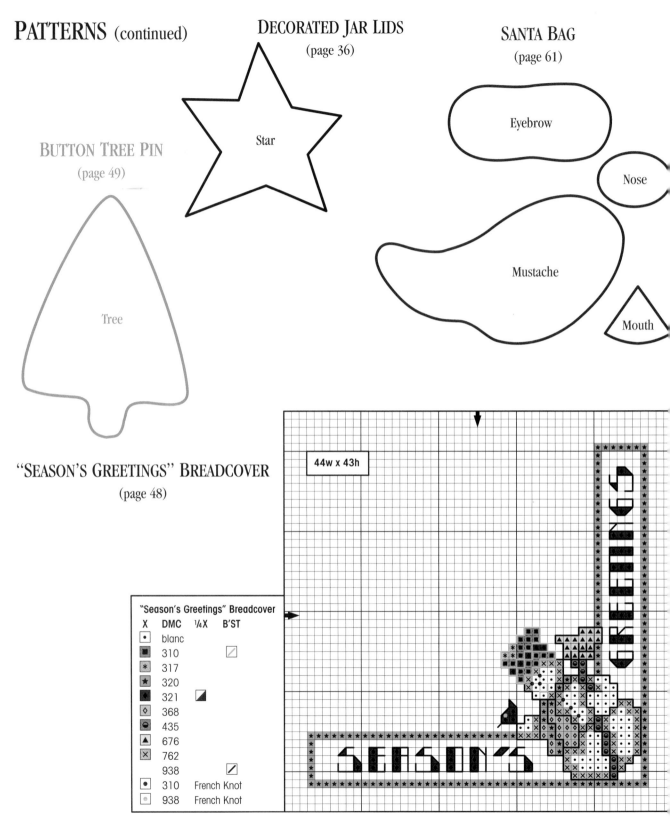

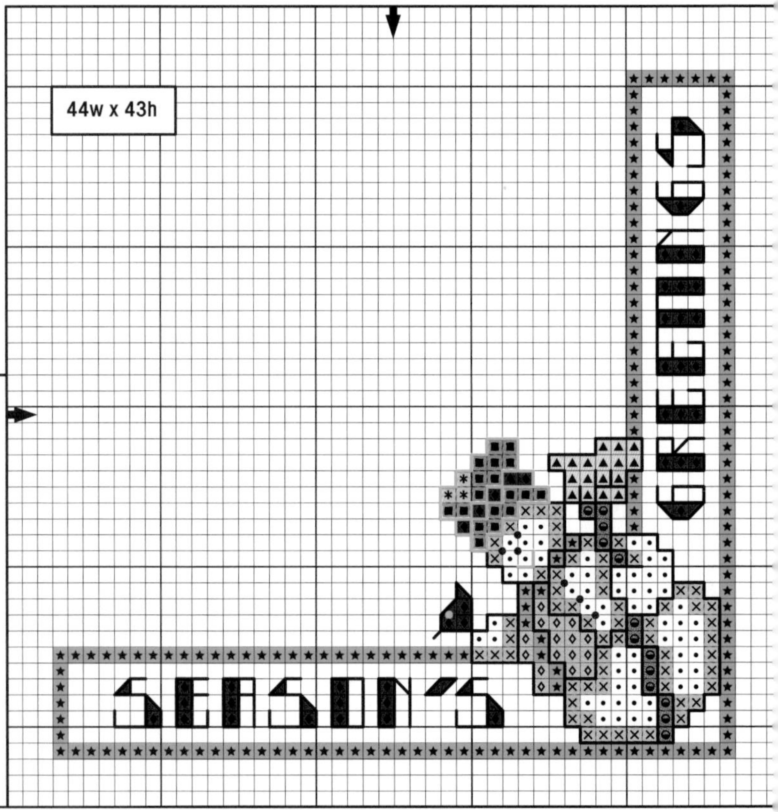
44w x 43h

"Season's Greetings" Breadcover

X	DMC	¼X	B'ST
•	blanc		
■	310		╱
✱	317		
★	320		
♦	321	◢	
◇	368		
◒	435		
▲	676		
✕	762		
	938		╱
●	310	French Knot	
●	938	French Knot	

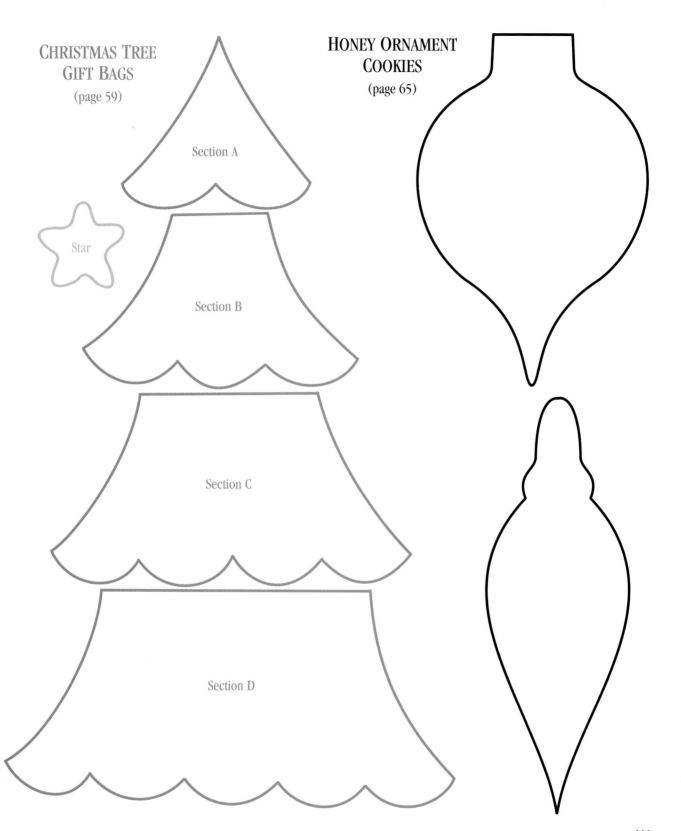

CHRISTMAS TREE
GIFT BAGS
(page 59)

Section A

Star

Section B

Section C

Section D

HONEY ORNAMENT
COOKIES
(page 65)

PATTERNS (continued)

STAR-BURST BREADCOVER
(page 63)

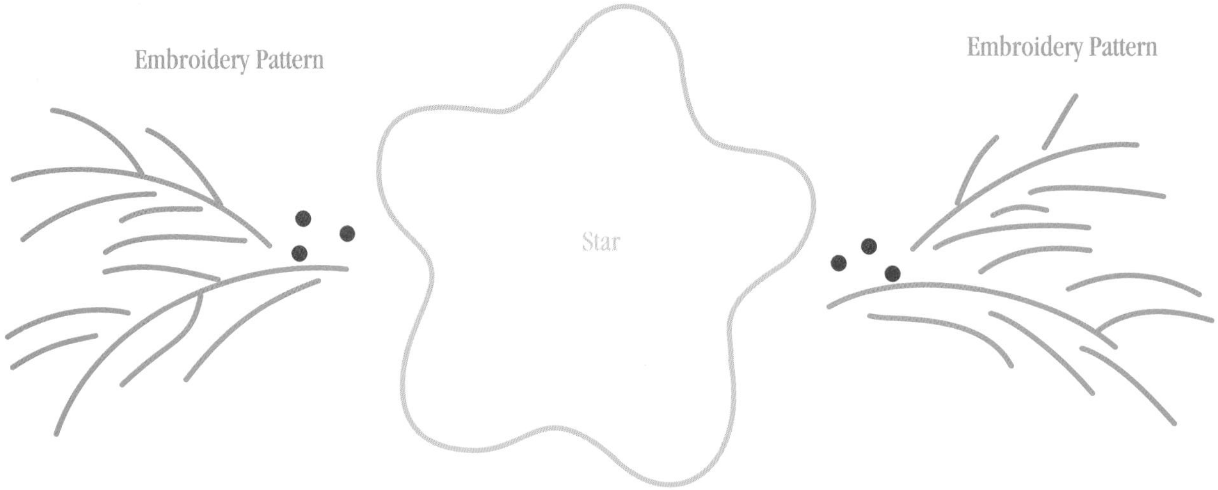

Embroidery Pattern

Embroidery Pattern

Star

SNOWFLAKE CAKE PLATE
(page 69)

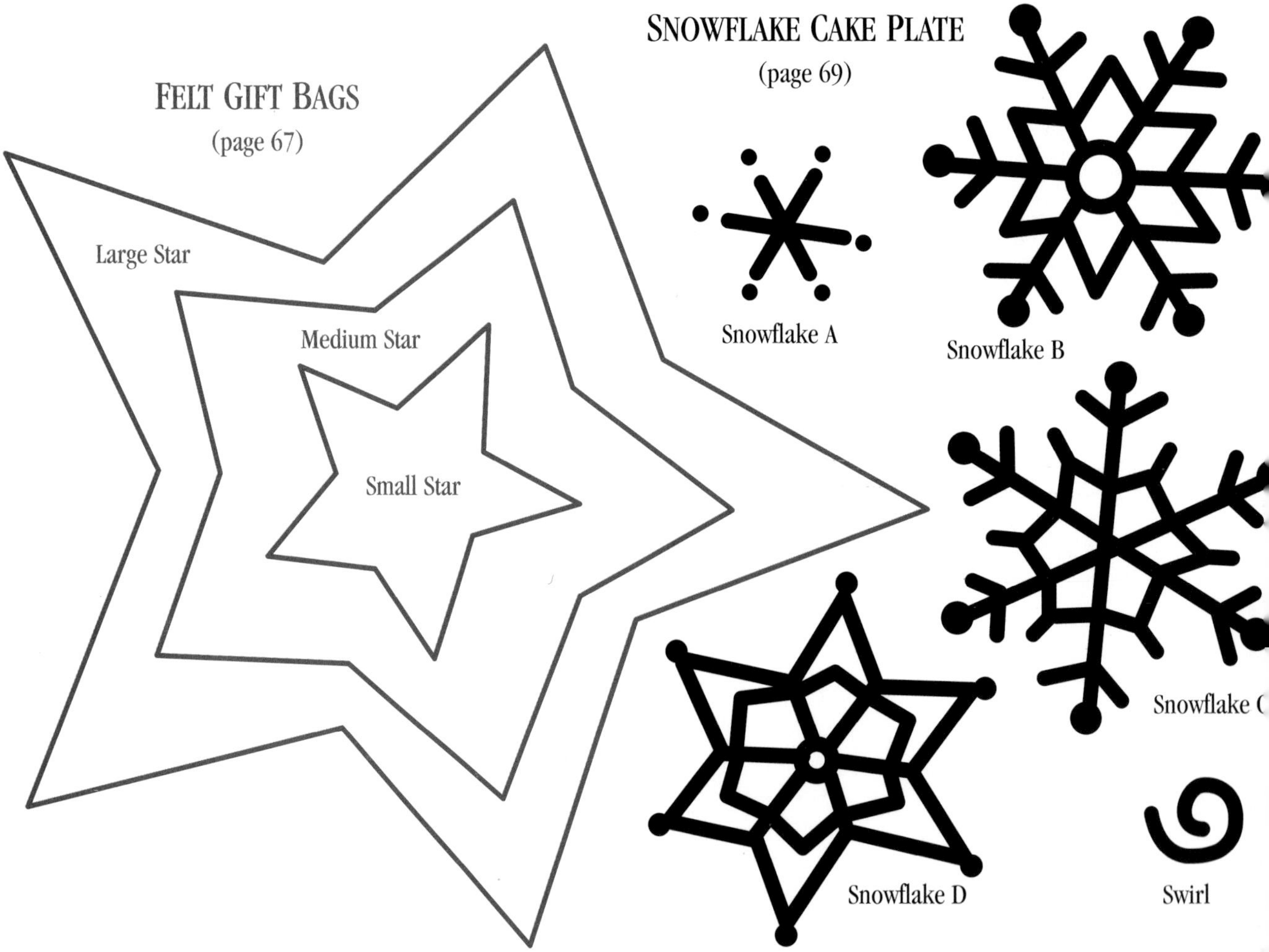

FELT GIFT BAGS
(page 67)

Large Star

Medium Star

Small Star

Snowflake A

Snowflake B

Snowflake C

Snowflake D

Swirl

Tag Designs

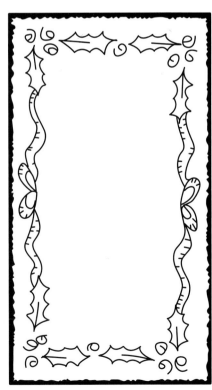

PATTERNS (continued)

SNOWMAN JAR
(page 79)

CINNAMON STICK REINDEER
(page 71)

Nose

Star

Head

Nose

Body

Ear

114

PEARS AND CREAM PIE
(page 80)

TIN-PUNCH PIE PAN
(page 80)

Holly Leaf

115

PATTERNS (continued)

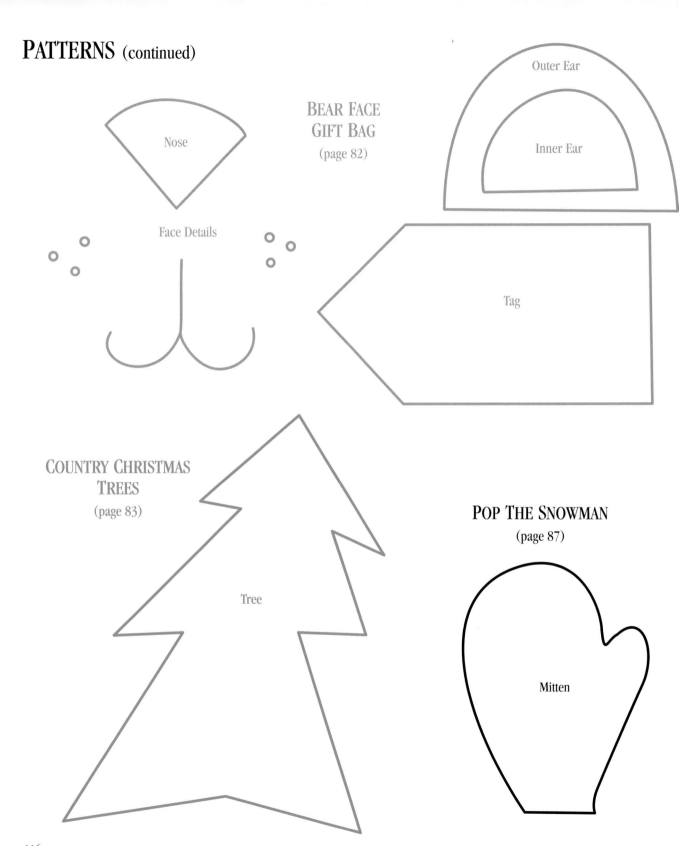

Nose

BEAR FACE
GIFT BAG
(page 82)

Outer Ear

Inner Ear

Face Details

Tag

COUNTRY CHRISTMAS
TREES
(page 83)

POP THE SNOWMAN
(page 87)

Tree

Mitten

DECORATED BASKET
AND JAR LID

(page 88)

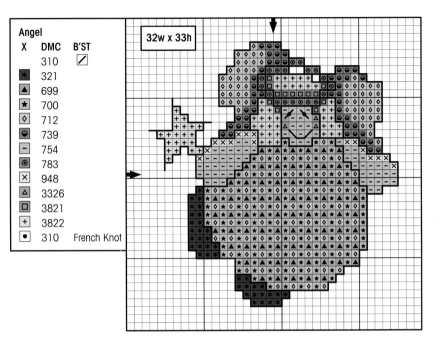

Angel

X	DMC	B'ST
	310	⟋
✳	321	
▲	699	
★	700	
◇	712	
◉	739	
−	754	
◉	783	
✕	948	
△	3326	
□	3821	
+	3822	
●	310	French Knot

32w x 33h

GIFT BAGS WITH
STOCKING MAGNETS

(page 90)

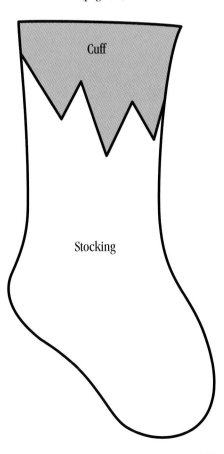

Cuff

Stocking

CHIMNEY GIFT BAG

(page 78)

SANTA stop here!

PATTERNS (continued)

CATNIP STOCKINGS
(page 91)

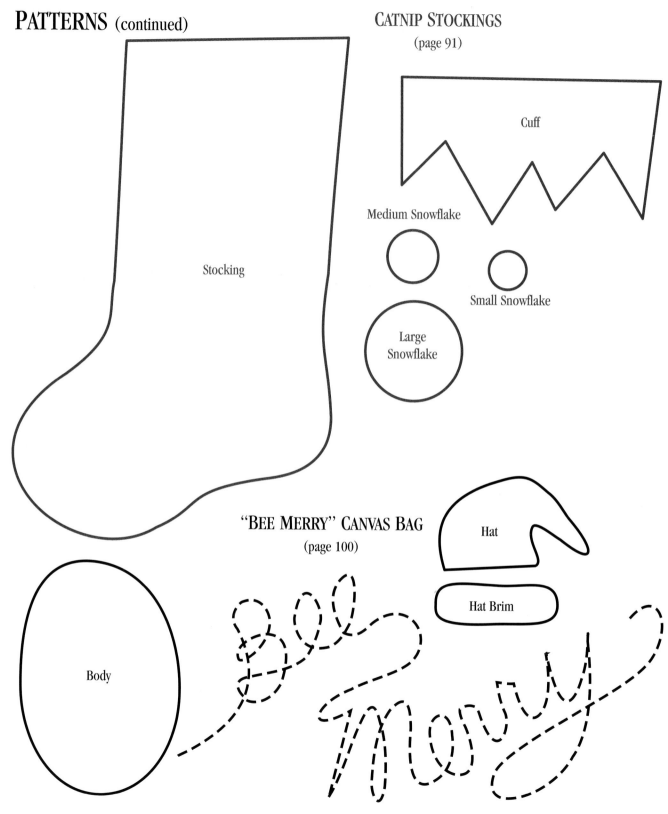

Stocking

Cuff

Medium Snowflake

Small Snowflake

Large Snowflake

"BEE MERRY" CANVAS BAG
(page 100)

Body

Hat

Hat Brim

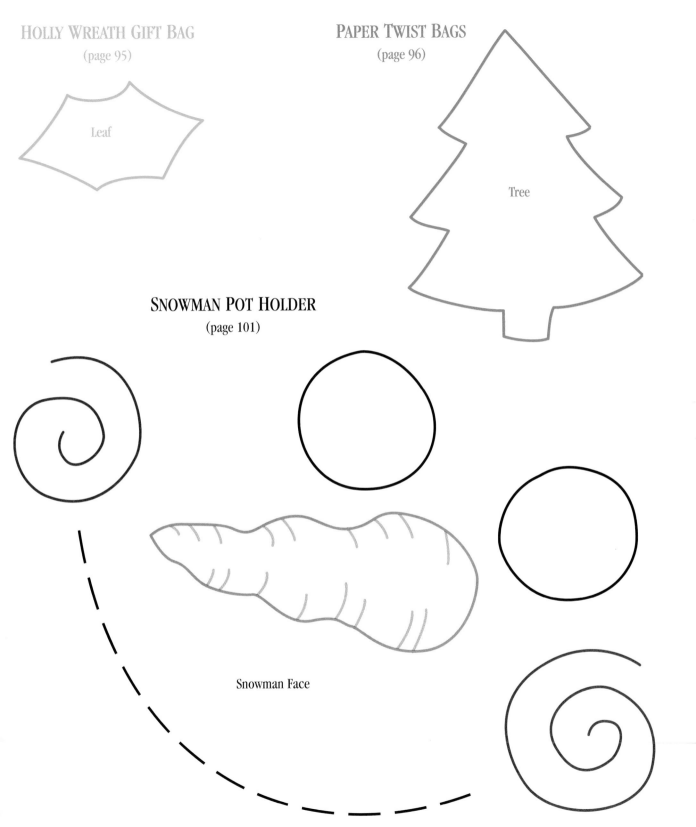

HOLLY WREATH GIFT BAG
(page 95)

Leaf

PAPER TWIST BAGS
(page 96)

Tree

SNOWMAN POT HOLDER
(page 101)

Snowman Face

PATTERNS (continued)

STOCKING APPLIQUÉ BAGS
(page 103)

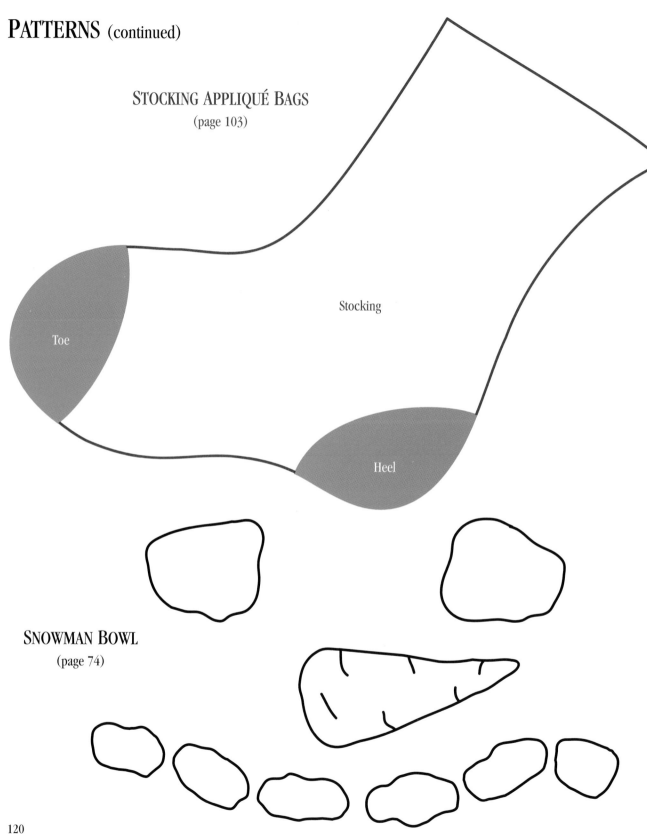

Stocking

Toe

Heel

SNOWMAN BOWL
(page 74)

GENERAL INSTRUCTIONS

ABOUT THE PAPER WE USED

For many of the projects in this book, we used white and colored paper. There are a variety of papers for these projects available at copy centers or craft stores. When selecting paper, choose one that is suitable in weight for the project. We used copier paper, card and cover stock, construction paper, poster board, bristol board, and handmade paper.

ABOUT ADHESIVES

Refer to the following list when selecting adhesives. Carefully follow the manufacturers' instructions when applying adhesives.

CRAFT GLUE: Recommended for paper, fabric, wood, and floral items. Dry flat or secure with clothespins or straight pins until glue is dry.

FABRIC GLUE: Recommended for fabric or paper items. Dry flat or secure with clothespins or straight pins until glue is dry.

HOT/LOW-TEMPERATURE GLUE GUN AND GLUE STICKS: Recommended for paper, fabric, and floral items; hold in place until set. Dries quickly. Low-temperature glue does not hold as well as hot glue, but offers a safer gluing option.

CRAFT GLUE STICK: Recommended for small, lightweight items. Dry flat.

SPRAY ADHESIVE: Recommended for adhering paper or fabric items. Dry flat.

RUBBER CEMENT: Recommended for adhering paper to paper; dries quickly.

DECOUPAGE GLUE: Recommended for applying fabric or paper pieces to smooth surfaces.

HOUSEHOLD CEMENT: Used for ceramic and metal items; secure until set.

TRACING PATTERNS

When entire pattern is shown, place tracing paper over pattern and trace pattern; cut out. For a more durable pattern, use a permanent pen to trace pattern onto stencil plastic; cut out.

When only half of pattern is shown (indicated by blue line on pattern), fold tracing paper in half and place fold along blue line of pattern. Trace pattern half; turn folded paper over and draw over traced lines on remaining side of paper. Unfold paper and cut out pattern. For a more durable pattern, use a permanent pen to trace pattern half onto stencil plastic; turn stencil plastic over and align blue lines to form a whole pattern. Trace pattern half again; cut out.

When patterns are stacked or overlapped, place tracing paper over pattern and follow a single colored line to trace pattern. Repeat to trace each pattern separately onto tracing paper.

MAKING A TAG

For a quick and easy tag, photocopy desired tag design and color with colored pencils or markers. Use straight-edge or decorative-edge craft scissors to cut out tag; glue to colored paper. Leaving a color border around tag, cut tag from colored paper. Use pen or marker to write message on tag.

For a fabric-backed tag, photocopy desired tag design and color with colored pencils or markers. Use straight-edge or decorative-edge craft scissors to cut out tag. Use pen or marker to write message on tag. Fuse a piece of paper-backed fusible web to wrong side of fabric. Fuse fabric to poster board. Glue tag to fabric-covered poster board. Leaving a fabric border around tag, cut out tag.

JAR LID FINISHING

1. For jar lid insert, use flat part of a jar lid (same size as jar lid used in storing food) as a pattern and cut one circle each from cardboard, batting, and fabric. Use craft glue to glue batting circle to cardboard circle. Center fabric circle right side up on batting; glue edges of fabric circle to batting.
2. Just before presenting gift, remove band from filled jar; place jar lid insert in band and replace band over lid.

MAKING A BOW

Loop sizes given in project instructions refer to the length of ribbon used to make one loop of bow.

1. For first streamer, measure desired length of streamer from one end of ribbon; twist ribbon between fingers (Fig. 1).

Fig. 1

2. Keeping right side of ribbon facing out, fold ribbon to front to form desired-size loop; gather ribbon between fingers (Fig. 2). Fold ribbon to back to form another loop; gather ribbon between fingers (Fig. 3).

Continued on page 122

GENERAL INSTRUCTIONS (continued)

Fig. 2   Fig. 3

 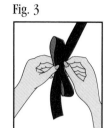

3. (*Note:* If a center loop is desired, form half the desired number of loops, then loosely wrap ribbon around thumb and gather ribbon between fingers as shown in Fig. 4; form remaining loops.) Continue to form loops, varying size of loops as desired, until bow is desired size.

Fig. 4

4. For remaining streamer, trim ribbon to desired length.

5. To secure bow, hold gathered loops tightly. Fold a length of floral wire around gathers of loops. Hold wire ends behind bow, gathering all loops forward; twist bow to tighten wire. Arrange loops and trim ribbon ends as desired.

PAINTING TECHNIQUES

TRANSFERRING A PATTERN

Trace pattern onto tracing paper. Using removable tape, tape pattern to project. Place transfer paper coated side down between project and tracing paper. Use a stylus or an old ball point pen that does not write to transfer outlines of basecoat areas of design to project (press lightly to avoid smudges and heavy lines that are difficult to cover). If necessary, use a soft eraser to remove any smudges.

PAINTING BASECOATS

A disposable foam plate makes a good palette.

Use a medium round brush for large areas and a small round brush for small areas. Do not overload brush. Allowing to dry between coats, apply several thin coats of paint to project.

TRANSFERRING DETAILS

To transfer detail lines to design, replace pattern and transfer paper over painted basecoats and use stylus to lightly transfer detail lines onto project.

ADDING DETAILS

Use a permanent pen to draw over detail lines.

SPONGE PAINTING

Use an assembly-line method when making several sponge-painted projects. Place project on a covered work surface. Practice sponge-painting technique on scrap paper until desired look is achieved. Paint projects with first color and allow to dry before moving to next color. Use a clean sponge for each additional color.

For allover designs, dip a dampened sponge piece into paint; remove excess paint on a paper towel. Use a light stamping motion to paint item.

For painting with sponge shapes, dip a dampened sponge shape into paint; remove excess paint on a paper towel. Lightly press sponge shape onto project. Carefully lift sponge. For a reverse design, turn sponge shape over.

MAKING APPLIQUÉS

Follow all steps for each appliqué. When tracing patterns for more than one appliqué, leave at least 1" between shapes on web.

To make a reverse appliqué, trace pattern onto tracing paper, turn traced pattern over, and follow all steps using traced pattern.

When an appliqué pattern contains shaded areas, trace along entire outer line for appliqué indicated in project instructions. Trace outer lines of shaded areas for additional appliqués indicated in project instructions.

1. Trace appliqué pattern onto paper side of web. (Some pieces may be given as measurements. Draw shape the measurements given in project instructions on paper side of web.) Cutting about 1/2" outside drawn lines, cut out web shape.

2. Follow manufacturer's instructions to fuse web shape to wrong side of fabric. Cut out shape along drawn lines.

MACHINE APPLIQUÉ

Set sewing machine for a medium-width zigzag stitch with a short stitch length. When using nylon or metallic thread for appliqué, use regular thread in bobbin.

1. Pin or baste a piece of stabilizer slightly larger than design to wrong side of background fabric under design area.

2. Beginning on straight edge of appliqué if possible, position fabric under presser foot so that most of the stitching will be on the appliqué piece. Holding upper thread toward you, sew over thread for

two to three stitches to prevent thread from raveling. Stitch over all exposed raw edges of appliqué(s) and along detail lines as indicated in project instructions.

3. When stitching is complete, remove stabilizer. Pull loose threads to wrong side of fabric; knot and trim ends.

MAKING A SEWN FABRIC BAG

1. To determine width of fabric needed, add ¹/₂" to desired finished width of bag. To determine length of fabric needed, double desired finished height of bag; add 1¹/₂". Cut a piece of fabric the determined measurements.

2. Matching right sides and short edges, fold fabric in half; finger press folded edge (bottom of bag). Using a ¹/₄" seam allowance, sew sides of bag together.

3. For bag with flat bottom, match each side seam to fold line at bottom of bag; sew across each corner 1" from point (Fig. 1).

Fig. 1

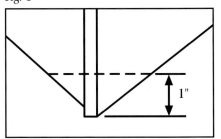

4. Press top edge of bag ¹/₄" to wrong side; press ¹/₂" to wrong side again and stitch in place.

5. Turn bag right side out.

MAKING A BASKET LINER

For liner with an unfinished edge, cut or tear a fabric piece ¹/₄" larger on all sides than desired finished size of liner. Fringe edges of fabric piece ¹/₄" or use pinking shears to trim edges.

For liner with a finished edge, cut a fabric piece ¹/₂" larger on all sides than desired finished size of liner. Press edges of fabric piece ¹/₄" to wrong side; press ¹/₄" to wrong side again and stitch in place.

CROSS STITCH

CROSS STITCH (X)

Work one Cross Stitch to correspond to each colored square in chart. For horizontal rows, work stitches in two journeys (Fig. 1). For vertical rows, complete each stitch as shown in Fig. 2.

Fig. 1

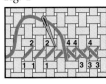

Fig. 2

BACKSTITCH (B'ST)

For outline detail, Backstitch (shown in chart and color key by black or colored straight lines) should be worked after design has been completed (Fig. 3).

Fig. 3

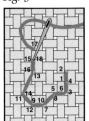

EMBROIDERY STITCHES

FRENCH KNOT

Bring needle up at 1 (Fig. 1); wrap floss once around needle and insert needle at 2, holding end of floss with non-stitching fingers. Tighten knot, then pull needle through fabric, holding floss until it must be released. For a larger knot, use more strands; wrap only once.

Fig. 1

RUNNING STITCH

Make a series of straight stitches with stitch length equal to the space between stitches (Fig. 2).

Fig. 2

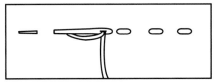

STRAIGHT STITCH

Bring needle up at 1 and go down at 2 (Fig. 3). Length of stitches may be varied as desired.

Fig. 3

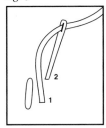

KITCHEN TIPS

MEASURING INGREDIENTS

Liquid measuring cups have a rim above the measuring line to keep liquid ingredients from spilling. Nested measuring cups are used to measure dry ingredients, butter, shortening, and peanut butter. Measuring spoons are used for measuring both dry and liquid ingredients.

To measure flour or granulated sugar: Spoon ingredient into nested measuring cup and level off with a knife. Do not pack down with spoon.

To measure confectioners sugar: Sift sugar, spoon lightly into nested measuring cup, and level off with a knife.

To measure brown sugar: Pack sugar into nested measuring cup and level off with a knife. Sugar should hold its shape when removed from cup.

To measure dry ingredients equaling less than 1/4 cup: Dip measuring spoon into ingredient and level off with a knife.

To measure butter, shortening, or peanut butter: Pack ingredient firmly into nested measuring cup and level off with a knife.

To measure liquids: Use a liquid measuring cup placed on a flat surface. Pour ingredient into cup and check measuring line at eye level.

To measure honey or syrup: For a more accurate measurement, lightly spray measuring cup or spoon with cooking spray before measuring so the liquid will release easily from cup or spoon.

TESTS FOR CANDY MAKING

To determine the correct temperature of cooked candy, use a candy thermometer and the cold water test. Before each use, check the accuracy of your candy thermometer by attaching it to the side of a small saucepan of water, making sure thermometer does not touch bottom of pan. Bring water to a boil. Thermometer should register 212 degrees in boiling water. If it does not, adjust the temperature range for each candy consistency accordingly.

When using a candy thermometer, insert thermometer into candy mixture, making sure thermometer does not touch bottom of pan. Read temperature at eye level. Cook candy to desired temperature range. Working quickly, drop about 1/2 teaspoon of candy mixture into a cup of ice water. Use a fresh cup of water for each test. Use the following descriptions to determine if candy has reached the correct consistency:

Soft-Ball Stage (234 to 240 degrees): Candy can be rolled into a soft ball in ice water but will flatten when removed from the water.

Firm-Ball Stage (242 to 248 degrees): Candy can be rolled into a firm ball in ice water but will flatten if pressed when removed from the water.

Hard-Ball Stage (250 to 268 degrees): Candy can be rolled into a hard ball in ice water and will remain hard when removed from the water.

Soft-Crack Stage (270 to 290 degrees): Candy will form hard threads in ice water but will soften when removed from the water.

Hard-Crack Stage (300 to 310 degrees): Candy will form brittle threads in ice water and will remain brittle when removed from the water.

SOFTENING BUTTER OR MARGARINE

To soften 1 stick of butter, remove wrapper and place butter on a microwave-safe plate. Microwave on medium-low power (30%) 20 to 30 seconds.

SOFTENING CREAM CHEESE

To soften cream cheese, remove wrapper and place cream cheese on a microwave-safe plate. Microwave on medium power (50%) 1 to 1 1/2 minutes for an 8-ounce package or 30 to 45 seconds for a 3-ounce package.

SHREDDING CHEESE

To shred cheese easily, place wrapped cheese in freezer 10 to 20 minutes before shredding.

USING CANDY COATING

To melt candy coating, place in top of a double boiler over hot, not simmering, water or in a heavy saucepan over low heat. Using a dry spoon, stir occasionally until coating melts. Remove from heat and use for dipping as desired. If coating begins to harden, return to heat. To flavor candy coating, add a small amount of flavored oil. To thin candy coating, add a small amount of vegetable oil; do not add water. To tint candy coating, use an oil-based food coloring.

MELTING CHOCOLATE

To melt chocolate, place chopped or shaved chocolate in top of a double boiler over hot, not simmering, water. Using a dry spoon, stir occasionally until chocolate melts. Remove from heat and use as desired. If chocolate begins to harden, return to heat.

TOASTING NUTS

To toast nuts, spread nuts on an ungreased baking sheet. Stirring occasionally, bake in a 350-degree oven 5 to 8 minutes or until nuts are slightly darker in color.

TOASTING COCONUT

To toast coconut, spread a thin layer of coconut on an ungreased baking sheet. Stirring occasionally, bake 5 to 7 minutes in a 350-degree oven or until coconut is lightly browned.

CUTTING OUT COOKIES

Place a piece of white paper or stencil plastic (available at craft stores) over pattern. Use a permanent felt-tip pen with fine point to trace pattern; cut out pattern. Place pattern on rolled-out dough and use a small, sharp knife to cut out cookies. (*Note:* If dough is sticky, frequently dip knife into flour while cutting out cookies.)

SUBSTITUTING HERBS

To substitute fresh herbs for dried, use 1 tablespoon fresh chopped herbs for $1/2$ teaspoon dried herbs.

EQUIVALENT MEASUREMENTS

1 tablespoon	=	3 teaspoons
$1/8$ cup (1 fluid ounce)	=	2 tablespoons
$1/4$ cup (2 fluid ounces)	=	4 tablespoons
$1/3$ cup	=	$5 1/3$ tablespoons
$1/2$ cup (4 fluid ounces)	=	8 tablespoons
$3/4$ cup (6 fluid ounces)	=	2 tablespoons
1 cup (8 fluid ounces)	=	16 tablespoons or $1/2$ pint
2 cups (16 fluid ounces)	=	1 pint
1 quart (32 fluid ounces)	=	2 pints
$1/2$ gallon (64 fluid ounces)	=	2 quarts
1 gallon (128 fluid ounces)	=	4 quarts

HELPFUL FOOD EQUIVALENTS

$1/2$ cup butter	=	1 stick butter
1 square baking chocolate	=	1 ounce chocolate
1 cup chocolate chips	=	6 ounces chocolate chips
$2 1/4$ cups packed brown sugar	=	1 pound brown sugar
$3 1/2$ cups unsifted confectioners sugar	=	1 pound confectioners sugar
2 cups granulated sugar	=	1 pound granulated sugar
4 cups all-purpose flour	=	1 pound all-purpose flour
1 cup shredded cheese	=	4 ounces cheese
3 cups sliced carrots	=	1 pound carrots
$1/2$ cup chopped celery	=	1 rib celery
$1/2$ cup chopped onion	=	1 medium onion
1 cup chopped green pepper	=	1 large green pepper

RECIPE INDEX

CREDITS

To Magna IV Color Imaging of Little Rock, Arkansas, we say *thank you* for the superb color reproduction and excellent pre-press preparation.

We want to especially thank photographers Larry Pennington, Mark Mathews, Ken West, and Karen Shirey of Peerless Photography, Little Rock, Arkansas, and Jerry R. Davis of Jerry Davis Photography, Little Rock, Arkansas, for their time, patience, and excellent work.

To the talented people who helped in the creation of the following recipes and projects in this book, we extend a special word of thanks:

- *Cross Stitch Jar Lid*, page 14: Deborah Lambein
- *Light Chocolate Eclair Dessert,* page 41: Karen Jackson
- *"Season's Greetings" Breadcover*, page 48: Deborah Lambein
- *Orange Slice Cake,* page 55: Audrey Gray
- *Cross Stitch Angel Ornament*, page 88: Karen Wood
- *Frozen Peach Torte,* page 89: Melissa Adams
- *Haystacks,* page 105: Jean Evans Pharr

Our sincere appreciation also goes to Vickie Barnes, Dena Duvall, Pat Johnson, and Angie Perryman, who assisted in making and testing some of the projects in this book.